Who Nee<

How to Write Funny Lyrics is both a crash course for the novice and a unique toolbox for the professional. It's full of useful angles and procedures that set it apart from other lyric writing manuals.

Non-musicians are sometimes called upon to supply the words for original musical numbers. Comedy writers, playwrights, actors and stand-up comics will find this guide a great help when a project requires funny lyrics.

Seasoned songwriters will appreciate the velocity with which certain basics are covered here. They are continually interwoven with the task at hand – creation of comic material.

This book isn't for kids; it's for witty, rather impatient adults. May it exploit your genius in mere minutes.

"Michael clearly shows how to access your comic instincts and turn ideas into well made lyrics."

Lee Costello
Executive Director
The Second City Los Angeles

Also by Michael Pollock

Musical Improv Comedy
Creating Songs in the Moment

"Michael Pollock has written a brilliantly detailed, scholarly, yet totally entertaining treatise on the unique art of creating the improvised song. His many years of tried and proven techniques are skillfully and clearly demonstrated. If you want to learn how to perform a great improv song, this book is a 'must.'"

Richard M. Sherman
Academy Award winning composer/lyricist
Mary Poppins, Jungle Book, Chitty Chitty Bang Bang and many more...

"Use it well, let it educate and excite you, free your imagination and your transition to actual performing will be seamless."

Jason Alexander
Tony Award winning actor
Jerome Robbins' Broadway

Musical Direction for Improv and Sketch Comedy

"There aren't a lot of shortcuts to great results, but one in particular happens to be this book."

Rick Overton
Emmy Award winning writer
Dennis Miller Live

"Michael Pollock's skill with improvised music for comedy is simply unsurpassed."

Jeff B. Davis
ABC's *Whose Line Is It Anyway?*

THANKS

TO THE CREATIVE ARTISTS WHO HELPED MAKE THIS BOOK

Sonja Alarr

Christopher Colley

Thomas Griep

Evelyn Halus

Tom Hippler

Marc Evan Jackson

Richard Martinez

David Razowsky

Michael Sherman

Jennifer Taylor

"WHAT A GIFT! The wonderful power of Michael's book is that it lays out in objective terms and practical games how to tackle something that can seem so subjective, so daunting and so terrifying – writing the words of a song. And then he shows you how to make it funny to boot!"

Pat Towne
Actor and co-founder of
The Annoyance Theater, Chicago

HOW TO WRITE FUNNY LYRICS
The Comedy Songwriting Manual

by Michael Pollock

MASTERYEAR
PUBLISHING
Hollywood, California

How to Write Funny Lyrics
The Comedy Songwriting Manual

By Michael Pollock

ISBN 0-9747427-2-4

Published by:
Masteryear Publishing
P. O. Box 69638
Los Angeles CA 90069 U.S.A.

Editor: Sonja Alarr
Cover design, illustration and layout: Michael Sherman
Back cover photo: Jennifer Taylor

Library of Congress Control Number: 2006925967
Pollock, Michael
How to Write Funny Lyrics: The Comedy Songwriting Manual

TABLE OF CONTENTS

Foreword

By David Razowsky

Okay, I never wanted to work at The Second City. Ever. Yeah, I was born and raised in Chicago, but working at that theatre wasn't for someone who had low self esteem, never considered themselves as funny as the next guy, and wasn't all that good looking.

Did I mention low self esteem?

So imagine my surprise when I auditioned for The Second City touring company in 1987 and was offered a job. I thought there must have been some kind of mistake, but I wasn't about to tell anyone.

The National Touring Company of The Second City performs "archival material," scenes that actors in resident companies have written throughout the theatre's wonderful history. In addition to the scenes, songs are a major element of the revues. Smart, funny, topical and surprising – the lyrics are hilarious. I always thought Second City had their musical directors write them. After all, they're the professional musicians.

Wrong! Just as the scenes are written by the actors, so are the songs, and you might never hear them outside of a theatre where a Second City performance is taking place. What other show might feature songs like these: a dramatic duet between American and Soviet generals; a tango celebrating rotisserie chicken at Boston Market; a love song praising the properties of helium, sung by two clowns; a lament about the inevitability of cancer, sung by old men on a bench?

The first song I wrote for a Second City revue was informative, smart and topical. Did I mention funny? I didn't have to, because it wasn't – and that's not just the low self esteem talking. Sheldon Patinkin, artistic consultant to The Second City, gave me some advice: "Make it funny."

Thanks, Sheldon.

At the time, I would have welcomed a book on how to write a funny, satirical song. That book has finally been written, and it's in your hands.

Michael's book doesn't just give great advice on how to write funny lyrics; he shows you how easy it is to open up your head and allow the funny stuff to come out. When he writes, "Comedy is born of surprise," he's saying that you must work to surprise yourself.

This book will help you find your voice, your personal point of view. Creating a funny song is about much more than rhyming; it's about releasing your judgment and letting what pours out, pour out.

At the end of the day, it's my love of the creative process that has kept me going all these years at The Second City. Michael's book offers a window into that process. His excellent examples are extremely helpful, as are his similes. My favorite is "It's actually better if the possibilities just roll around in front of your nose like lottery balls." With advice like that, you can't lose.

Dare to fail and you won't.

Now get out there and make it funny.

David Razowsky
Artistic Director
The Second City Los Angeles

David Razowsky is in great demand as a director and teacher of master classes. He has written, directed and performed in Second City shows all over the U.S., as well as having directed two shows for Boom Chicago in Amsterdam. He can be reached at dlrkmm@pacbell.net.

1

What If the President Had a Lounge Act?

How to Develop an Idea for a Funny Song

I'm going to show you how to fish for funny. As you read this, countless comedy writers are having discussions based entirely around "What if?"

What if…there was an organization for everyone named Mike? There is! It's called Mikes of America. What if they had a theme song?

Follow my lead as we search around in reality for funny song ideas – just "true stuff" to begin with.

If you think something is funny, you probably won't be alone, although you may sometimes be the first person who sees it that way and creates a product that entertains – what a great gift to the world! People need to laugh; it's more of an essential than a luxury. "What if…?" is a sacred preamble to potential joy for many. Our cause is noble.

Let's start.

WHAT'S YOUR SONG ABOUT?

Think of some **things that you simply like or dislike** – be honest. Can we possibly glean from these some amusing subject matter for the lyrics of a song? We're simply saying "I like this" or "I dislike that," and "what if one sang about it?" Imagine that.

Here is a short list of **things I like:**

Pugs
Martinis
Sushi
Giving parties
Playing the piano at Disneyland
Cheese (on just about everything)
Eating in restaurants
Staying in hotels
Sugar
My cell phone

We're in search of an idea that is born in truth. Later we can elaborate upon and amplify what may be ridiculous about it. Here's another list – **things I dislike:**

Working out
People who are always late
Obligatory Christmas shopping
Playing the piano at Disneyland (yes, it's on both lists)
Being bald
Rich kids – even though they can't help it
People who drive offensively
Junk mail
Voice Jail (touch tone response systems)
Cleaning out the refrigerator

Does the "dislike" category seem slightly juicier? Well, it is. Bemoaning a thing lends itself to funny because humor is a welcome pain reliever. What's more hilarious at times than finding common ground upon which to complain, and making a party of it? It's therapeutic.

Again, we're simply looking for subject matter to expand upon for our funny-lyric purposes – what *if* a guy sang a song about what a drag it is being bald? Could that be entertaining? Perhaps – might be fun to approach it ironically.* Sounds funny to me!

Let's move on to anger. **Think about things that make you mad.** These will resemble things that make you sad, but don't bum out – have some caffeine; choose aggression.

Possible targets for your rage:

> Identity theft
> Corporate crime
> Gangs
> Dishonest politicians
> Nasty neighbors
> Racism

These things are not funny, but could they be? Are they food for comedy? Very possibly…remember, we're going to fight back by seeking out the ridiculous. The more absurd or outrageous the truth, the less work we actually have to do. We're going to make fun of something by holding up a mirror to it – perhaps a bit of a fun-house mirror, but a mirror, nevertheless.

---

*Irony: To say one thing and mean another, i.e., *"I just spent a marvelous weekend stranded in Newark."* In this sense irony is like sarcasm. It can also refer to an unexpected outcome – medieval people thought that bathing would harm them, when in fact it led to the unsanitary conditions that caused the plague…ironic!

With any idea, we'll always endeavor to answer the question
– **Who might sing this song, and why?** This will help us to
proceed.

WHO SINGS THE SONG?

Often the answer to this is simply: any person who holds the viewpoint expressed in the lyrics. For example, the song is called "I'm
God's Gift to the Ladies," and the singer is (drum roll…) that
guy. You could go farther and identify him as a cowboy or a New
Yorker or what-have-you, which would help focus the viewpoint and
character of your lyrics.

If a song is a humorous story told in the third-person ("The Ballad
of Stephanie McGee"), it will be helpful to decide who's telling the
story…her dad? Her lover? Could be Stephanie herself, or just
some troubadour who knows the story.

When you're making fun of a particular person, viewpoint, custom,
habit or institution, realize that it's a great idea to have your lyrics
delivered by:

> A. that person
> B. a person with that viewpoint
> C. a person with that custom or habit
> D. a member of that institution

Knocking a political group? Have a flock of them sing the song.
Maybe one of your "dislikes" is "smokers." I enthusiastically suggest that it's a smoker who sings your song, if not eight of them.

WHY?

What is the reason for a song to be sung? It could be to justify behavior; to inform the world; to vent emotion; to plea for understanding; to cry out to the cosmos; to rally the masses; to set the record straight…when you're working with an idea, just ask yourself "why the song?" If it's a good idea, you'll have a ready answer.

When we poke fun at someone in their own voice the lyrics will demonstrate that our target deserves to be mocked. This will be a delight for the audience to behold – a brand of satire, defined below.

SATIRE

A literary technique through which ideas, customs, behaviors or institutions are ridiculed for the purpose of improving society. Satire may be gently witty, mildly abrasive or bitterly critical. It uses exaggeration and humor for effect.

The Unexpected is Funny

Now let's consider another route to a good idea. Think of any familiar entity that could sing a song as an individual or group, including non-humans…freely allow fantasy into the picture. Here are some examples:

The Mormon Tabernacle Choir	Cops
The President	Children
Computers	A librarian
Aliens	A Ku Klux Klansman
Dogs	Samurai warriors

Next, we work with them by putting unlikely or inconceivable words in their mouths. Those words will of course be the lyrics of a song. Imagine odd situations. We want to create an incongruous or silly picture. What would "never happen?" (Hint – you can always start with something conceivable but weird, then see where that leads you.) Examples:

1. *The Mormon Tabernacle Choir* will never present an evening of Pearl Jam hits. They will also never do "Java Jive," since Mormons abstain from caffeine. What else would they not do, in terms of singing an original song? ...A benefit concert for Planned Parenthood.

2. *The President* would never have a lounge act. So unlikely, even if Bill Clinton did play sax in public. What if the State of the Union address were presented in song, live from Laughlin, Nevada? His backup singers could be secret service guys – the "Ovalaires."

3. If *computers* could sing, what would they sing? We're already in the realm of incredulity, so this is a large playing field. How about a song about knowing all your private stuff (credit card numbers, email, chat, personal ads, web site views)...a "we've got the goods on you" kind of number?

4. *Aliens* singing is not so fantastic, since we probably think of them as beings who can walk, talk, eat, and...sing. A song about being held captive in Area 51 could be mildly interesting, but what would be more unexpected? I suggest they sing about "how tough it is to be telepathic." How can you have a romance with no mystery?

5. *Dogs* will be rather funny as they sing anything; we just need to paint a picture that smacks of as much surprise as possible. (My friends Milt Larsen and Richard Sherman wrote an entire musical called *Dawgs*, including songs like "Cuddle Me" and "Nobody Loves a Chihuahua." Very funny songs; however, we can go farther out on a limb.) My idea for this one: dogs singing a "euthanasia protest song" at the pound. There's a guitar and harmonica involved, and they all sound like Bob Dylan or Joan Baez.

6. *Cops* have a rough gig. They would probably never serenade us with "Don't Worry, Be Happy." We want to design an original song for them to sing, so we have to imagine a point of view or situation that's absurd. I see them surrounding a crack house, singing a "this is your last chance" song through bullhorns, as a doo-wop quartet. I know I'm getting elaborate here – I encourage you to go a little crazy.

7. It's funny when *children* say things that children wouldn't say, since they're supposed to be naïve. In the musical, *Ruthless*, the 8-year old main character belts out the wistful standard ballad, "I Stayed Too Long at the Fair" as she auditions for the school play. It's hilarious because it's so "wrong" for a little girl to be singing this very mature song. *Or you can, of course, portray kids as naïve*: in a recent Second City show we had actors playing children sing a song called "The NSA Sounds A-OK to Me," which was a play on their innocence, a la "surveillance is my friend!"*

*National Security Agency; if you didn't already know this you may want to look into it. They know quite a lot about YOU.

8. While any kind of person can be a *librarian*, there is such a thing as the prim, female, bespectacled stereotype that will survive for awhile, so let's have a trio of them shock the crowd as they perform a strip tease song and dance about the virtues of reading.

9. A *Ku Klux Klansman* would not lead us in singing "We Are the World." For an original song, what about a laundry detergent commercial – an extended musical jingle? Who better to glorify whiter whites?

10. *Samurai warriors* are not known for their choral offerings or their Broadway credits. I suggest they sing a big, smiley song and use their swords as canes while they offer a cheery "Hey, how ya doin', nobody-realizes-how-much-fun-we-can-be" tap number.

Comedy is always born in surprise, right? Ideas that come from consideration of the implausible can result in very funny lyrics.

As you can see among examples 1-10 above, such an approach may often incline itself toward a particular musical style. Great! When you go beyond basic subject matter for a song and conceive a bigger picture, more details will naturally become part of the idea.

More Possibilities

In this section I'll give you some additional angles for song ideas, along with examples of well known, funny songs that match the perspective. If you're unfamiliar with the examples, keep an ear out and listen to them when you can; you'll find them instructive.

A personal need, wish or predicament is a great launching pad. This might be something autobiographical, completely imaginary, or customized to fit a character in a show. Examples:

> "My Girlfriend Who Lives in Canada" from *Avenue Q*
> (I need to convince someone I'm not gay.)

> "The King of Broadway" from *The Producers*
> (I long to once again be a successful producer.)

> "I Cain't Say No" from *Oklahoma!*
> (What can I say? I'm a loose woman.)

> "A Boy Named Sue" by Shel Silverstein – recorded by Johnny Cash
> (I was cursed with this name, and here's my saga.)

Songs that give advice can be quite witty. A singer with some certain authority tells another person – or the audience – how to solve their problem. Examples:

> "You Gotta Get a Gimmick" from *Gypsy*
> (Here's how to be a successful stripper.)

> "Just Leave Everything to Me" from *Hello Dolly!*
> (No matter what you need, I'm the one you should call.)

> "Beauty School Dropout" from *Grease*
> (Your life isn't working; you need to switch gears.)

You may want your lyrics to **simply tell a funny story.** In that event you need a yarn with which to work, real or conjured. Here are some successful songs that have spun an entertaining, third-person narrative:

> "Grandma Got Run Over by a Reindeer" by Randy Brooks
> (A crazy account of a tragic accident)

"Harper Valley P.T.A." by Tom T. Hall
(A girl's mother reads the Riot Act to hypocritical residents of a small town.)

"Rocky Raccoon" by The Beatles
(A quirky old-west tale of infidelity and vengeance)

"Itsy Bitsy, Teenie Weenie, Yellow Polka Dot Bikini"
by Vance/Pockriss
(A girl is embarrassed to be seen in her new, skimpy swimwear.)

Funny songs sometimes **state a problem** or **ask a question concerning a problem.** Examples:

"Your Feet's Too Big" by Fats Waller
(This presents a number of difficulties.)

"Sam, You Made the Pants Too Long" by Lewis/Young/
Whitehouse/Berle
(I love the way you tailored my suit, except for this one thing...)

"Why Can't the English Learn to Speak?" from *My Fair Lady*
(It's atrocious what goes on linguistically around here, wot, wot?)

A great many songs have been written to **entertain children** – lullabies, affectionate songs, songs that teach good habits or tell a very tall tale...here are a few that I've written myself:

"All Aboard for Sleepytown"
(Better hop on or you won't get any rest.)

"That's How Long I'll Love You"
("I'll love you 'til the lolli-pops, the honey combs and the flower shops...")

Ideas for a song that will make an audience laugh can come from anywhere in your brilliant mind...not solely as a result of the methods we've outlined, although these do work! On occasion you might be just handed a concept – *a Feng Shui master sings a song* – with the assignment, "Come up with some comic lyrics." This book will prepare you to do that.

Turn Your Idea into a Title

Let's say that we have an idea. It has appeared from somewhere, and we're going to forge ahead with it. What now?

Next we **create a working title** – one that may change later, but will give us something to go on. Why not make the title sound like this *must* be a funny song?

All the well known titles we've looked at so far have filled this bill. Check out these additional examples:

> "I've Got Those 'God Why Don't You Love Me? Oh, you do? I'll See You Later' Blues"
> by Stephen Sondheim

> "The Masochism Tango" by Tom Lehrer

> "My Ding-A-Ling" by Chuck Berry

> "I'm Henry the Eighth, I Am" by Murray/Weston

> "I Need Your Help, Barry Manilow" by Dale Gonyea

When we eventually compose complete lyrics, we'll make use of the title within a song...so we need something that can function as a prominent line *in* a song. The 5 titles above work exactly that way in the songs they represent.

Rhymed words ("Silly Billy"), **clichés** ("The Jig is Up") and **alliteration** ("I'm a Ding Dong Daddy from Dumas") can serve beautifully. We don't need to be hilarious, just a little zany. Make sure that a title holds up as a "slogan" for what the whole song is about.

Let's create a few working titles for song ideas that have appeared previously in this chapter:

> Idea: I like martinis.
> "Two Ain't Enough, Three is Too Many"
>
> Idea: I dislike obligatory Christmas shopping.
> "The Holy Holiday Hold-up"
>
> Idea: Identity theft makes me mad.
> "Gee, it's Great to be You" (sung by an identity thief)
>
> Idea: Dogs sing a euthanasia protest song.
> "Yappin' at the Pearly Gates"
>
> Idea: Librarians do a strip tease song about the virtues of reading.
> "A Real Good Book'll Keep You Up All Night"
>
> Idea: Samurai warriors present a big, smiley tap number and song.
> "Howdy Hai, We're Samurai!"

I encourage you to browse back through the song-idea possibilities and theorize titles, or even better — come up with ideas and working titles of your own.

Imagine the Perfect Performer

It will help our entire process to visualize an appropriately odd or crazy character delivering the performance of a song. There's an old saying that goes:

"Comics say funny things; comedians say things funny."

No matter how clever your lyrics, your fervent desire should be for a *comedian* to sing them in order to get the most laughs possible. And of course, we want those lyrics to rise to the occasion of a fine comedy artist!

Now that we've explored numerous routes to good ideas, let's turn our attention to the words of a song.

2 They Laughed at My Poem — Thank God!

All You Need to Know About Rhyming

Rhyming is easy and fun. If you're a songwriter and already know every possible thing about it, read this just to make me happy.

Rhymes 101

Not all songs feature rhymes; only 99.9 percent of them. In terms of funny songs, the figure is closer to 100. Absorb this little chapter and you'll know plenty about how to accomplish the task.

Here are four categories of rhymed words. Each is based on the number of syllables we rhyme:

Single rhymes – accent on the last (or only) syllable:

    Dream / Cream   Believe / Conceive

Double rhymes – accent on the next-to-last syllable:

    Ceiling / Feeling   Delicious / Suspicious

Triple rhymes – accent on the third-to-last syllable:

Amorous / Glamorous   Fallopian / Utopian

Quadruple rhymes – accent on the fourth-to-last syllable:

Delusionary   Illusionary

The rhymed words above happen to possess identical numbers of syllables, which is fine, but not essential. We can be freer than that, using words containing dissimilar numbers of syllables, or even using word groups, provided we get the desired accent match for a single, double, triple or quadruple rhyme.

It doesn't matter how many total syllables a word contains, preceding the ones we want to rhyme:

PreCOcious (double-rhymes with)

SupercalifragilisticexpialaDOcious

In the rhyming columns of words below, notice: (1) accented and unaccented sounds that rhyme, and (2) what kind of rhyme has been created – single, double, triple or quadruple?

RING	Martin Luther **KING**
JOHN	Genghis **KHAN**
HAMmered	E**NAM**ored
DOing	Pooh-**POOHing**
Vi**RILL**ity	Affa**BIL**ity
Eth**NI**city	Eccen**TRI**city
Mag**NAN**imously	U**NAN**imously
DEAR	Cash**MERE**
LENtil	Judg**MEN**tal
HOLlywood	**BOL**lywood

The above sounds rhyme perfectly. We will, however, sometimes settle for "looser rhymes" like the following:

More	Bored
Key	Scene
Go	Road
Kalamazoo	Gather the crew
Recipient	Immigrant
Come	Done

We won't be quite as proud of them, but they'll slide into the occasional pinch.

Rhyme Schemes

I'm about to show you a rhyming pattern, called a rhyme scheme. Some kind of rhyme scheme will be present in the words of every song we write. In the following example we're going to label the conclusion of each line of lyrics with a letter – A, B, or C:

1. Mary had a little <u>lamb</u>
   (Call the sound at the end of this line **A**)

2. Its fleece was white as <u>snow</u>
   (Call this **B**, because it's different than **A**.)

3. And everywhere that Mary <u>went</u>
   (This is **C**, because it doesn't sound like **A** or **B**.)

4. The lamb was sure to <u>go</u>
   (Call this is **B** again, because *go* matches *snow*.)

That's an ABCB rhyme scheme.

Wait a Minute, Can We Make This Funny?

Sure. For fun, let's replace the "B" lines with new ones.

> *Mary had a little lamb*
> **She called "Marie-Collette"**
> *And everywhere that Mary went*
> **It nibbled a baguette**

The parody* above is slightly more entertaining. We're heading in the direction of comedy. Let's do it again, and end more strongly.

> *Mary had a little lamb*
> **She called "Marie-Collette"**
> *And everywhere that Mary went*
> **It sneered, "I'm no one's pet!"**

That one is better because it's a bigger surprise...starting to be funny. Let's punch it up one more time, making the last line as unexpected as possible:

> *Mary had a little lamb*
> **She called "Marie-Collette"**
> *And everywhere that Mary went*
> **It bummed a cigarette**

As we begin to create 4-line sections from scratch, we'll frequently try and make the final line the most clever, unanticipated or outrageous. On some occasions we'll make that 4th line a main idea that we keep driving home, again and again.

---

*Parody: An imitation of an existing, well known work, usually for the purpose of spoofing or satirizing it.

Building an ABCB Rhyme Scheme with Original Comedy

We will now prepare to write two 4-line sections of brand new lyrics. We can choose any subject; how about "Garbage?" Why garbage? Why not? This could have come from our list of "dislikes" in Chapter 1.

(Maybe we're contributing material to a musical revue that points to our use-it-and-toss-it society from myriad angles, and the producers have come to us for comic content.)

We need to create a **working title** that will inspire us to write lyrics. To accomplish this, spend a few moments with any mental images you have, relating to garbage. Be patient; there will be more than you thought...let one thing lead to another and just stop the wheel somewhere that seems like a hoot.

I suggest: "I've Got a Crush on the Trash Guys."

Now to roll up our sleeves...make a list of words, expressions or short word groups that have to do with the subject. We'll call this our general word bank.

General Word Bank

Trash	Waste	Throw out	Chuck it
Sanitation	Dirty	Dump	Odor
Rats	Food	Hefty Bag	Disposable
Messy	Junk	Smell	Ooze
Stinky	Throw away	Disgusting	"Gar-BAHJZ"

This list could be longer or shorter, depending on the task at hand. The words above are plenty for us to work with right now.

Next, we will **take these words and come up with a healthy number of rhymes for each of them.** It's worthwhile effort, as it will make our entire job much easier. Feel free to use a rhyming dictionary! Don't trouble yourself with alphabetizing your own lists – you won't think up every rhyming word in alphabetical order, and it's actually better if the possibilities just roll around in front of your nose like lottery balls. Here we go...

Word Bank Rhymes

(Always check to see if any of your main words already rhyme with each other.)

Trash: stash, cash, dash, flash, hash, rash, bash, panache, brash
Sanitation: situation, fluctuation, mastication, emancipation, railway station, altercation
Rats: hats, gnats, flats, cats, bats, tatts, frats, stats
Messy: Bessie, dressy, Jesse
Stinky: dinky, kinky, pinky, slinky, Twinkie
Waste: taste, maced, distaste, haste, laced, faced, disgraced
Dirty: flirty, "purty," (or more loosely...birdie, wordy, sturdy, Princess "Fergie")
Food: lewd, rude, construed, cooed, mood, prude, dude, feud, exude, intrude
Junk: trunk, stunk, flunk, bunk, funk, dunk, sunk
Throw away: go away, flow away, blow away, stowaway, row away, go astray
Throw out: go out, blow out, show out, flow out, grow out
Dump: slump, pump, rump, hump, bump, plump, frump, lump
Hefty bag: No rhymes, but it might come in handy all by itself – resist "lefty hag."

Smell: bell, tell, shell, mademoiselle, fell, quell, hell, Muscatel
Disgusting: rusting, dusting, busting, combusting, lusting
Chuck it: duck it, suck it, tuck it, buck it (yeah, and that other one)
Odor: loader, Schroeder, motor, loader, coder, decoder
Disposable: closable, decomposable, hose a bull (lame, admittedly)
Ooze: snooze, booze, fuse, use, news, muse, peruse, zoos, pooh-poohs
"Gar-BAHJZ:" mirage, collage (loose – decoupage, triage)

As a reward for our sweat, we now have both a title and a lot of relevant rhyming ammunition. Excellent.

For this short project, let's make the title the first line of each set of 4 lines.

1. *I've got a crush on the trash guys*

We're off and running. Let's break for lunch.

Okay, we're back.

Take a look into the Word Bank Rhymes and **find a word pair that might be a good team.** Our title is romantic. We peruse and we see that *lusting* rhymes with *disgusting*... *suck it* rhymes with *chuck it*... *food* rhymes with *lewd* and *prude*...we're looking for stuff that seems to have to do with love, or you know, "desire."

There's also *go out* (like go out on a date)...which we see rhymes with *throw out.* And *kinky* rhymes with *stinky.* Let's pick that last pair and give this a try.

We must now **decide which of these two words might work best as the payoff** – the rhyme fulfilling, last word of a 4-line section.

I'd say it could easily be either one – kinky or stinky, but "kinky" is probably the most interesting. We now have this:

1. I've got a crush on the trash guys

2. <u>blah blah blah blah</u> **stinky**

3. <u>blah blah blah blah, BLAH blah blah blah</u>

4. <u>blah blah blah blah</u> **kinky**

We're doing well, even though a certain amount of staring at blank lines remains. We've begun a perfectly good lyric story and built in rhyming words, the second of which will function nicely as a surprise for the audience. "Kinky" will be our little kicker, which some busty comedienne will sing with a bump and a grind.

Now it's time to **examine the lines in order,** 1-4, and fill in the blank areas with logical statements. Logic is paramount – we want to make sense all the way through, and if we've done our job well up to this point, it shouldn't be too difficult.

Line One is the jump start: the clearer its message, the better. Here's a possibility:

> *I've got a crush on the trash guys*
> *Even though they're stinky*
> *Every time that truck pulls up*
> *I feel a little kinky*

Is this brilliant? Don't even worry about it; just be happy something got written. A flow has begun!

If we were making up lyrics for an entire song, we'd end up with quite a few that would be later thrown out...we'd switch things around...we'd discover that the first thing we wrote actually worked best at the very end of the song, but with a brand new rhyme that came to us the next morning...the important thing right now is to use our tools and CREATE.

Back to the game – we're going to do an additional 4 lines, so we refer again to the list of Word Bank Rhymes. Suddenly, *throw away* and *stowaway* seem intriguing, so let's plug those into the next puzzle:

1. I've got a crush on the trash guys

2. _____throw away

3. _____

4. _____ stowaway

Note that I chose "stowaway" as the payoff word. More unexpected than "throw away," don't you think? That's why I put it at the end.

Again, we now take each line in sequence and see if we can fill in the blanks with thoughts that make sense. How about this:

> *I've got a crush on the trash guys*
> <u>*Who haul off what I*</u> *throw away*
> <u>*I wanna curl up in a Hefty bag*</u>
> <u>*And be their dirty*</u> *stowaway*

The lyrics continue kinkily. Sorry, this isn't your grandma's book of silly words for songs.

Throwing in "hefty bag" and "dirty" contribute to the garbage-ness of it all. Apart from the task of rhyming, we can **draw upon the general word bank for thematic vocabulary**.

Additional Rhyme Schemes

Now I'll show you examples of some other rhyme schemes we'll be employing along the way. I'm going to create these examples by choosing likely pairs of words that rhyme, and placing them at the ends of the appropriate lines.

1. My mother would find it dis**gusting**   A

2. If she knew the details of my **lusting**   A

3. I'd be spurned, cast out and **disgraced**   B

4. If she learned of my love, "gone to **waste**"   B

1. It's only a dream situ**ation**   A

2. Maybe it's nothing but **bunk**   B

3. But whenever I think "sani**tation**"   A

4. My heart wants to follow the **junk**   B

1. Late in the evening, **alone**   A

2. I think about things that are **messy**   B

3. Stains on those work gloves that **smell**   C

4. Like some old wino's ditched Musca**tel**   C

All the rhymes we've worked with so far are called **end rhymes**, meaning that they are positioned at the ends of lines. When words within any line rhyme each other as well, we call those **internal rhymes**. Here's an example of an internal rhyme in Line 3:

1. Yes, I've got a crush on the **trash guys**   A

2. So I'm pitching my tent at the **dump**   B

3. I don't care if it's **rude**; call me nasty or **lewd**,   C

4. But that's where I'm parking my **rump**   B

It's a matter of how hard you want to work at rhyming. The ABCB rhyme scheme is simplest to accomplish; beyond that, do what you wish. Audiences love the cleverness of rhymes galore, and comedy songs will sometimes feature a great many because it's just so silly. Behold:

"Moses supposes his Toe-ses are Roses, but Moses supposes erroneously!"
Singin' in the Rain

Now that you know how rhyme schemes work, you can create any kind you want: AAAA, ABAB, AABB, ABAA, ABBA...

There Once was a Girl from Nantucket...

Limericks have long amused the public. Let's take a quick look at what's going on there:

> There was a young lady named *Maud*
> Who was the most terrible *fraud*
> She never was *able* to eat at the *table*
> But when in the kitchen, Oh *Gawd*!
> - Unknown

As you can see – the limerick above contains 4 lines, an AABA rhyme scheme, an internal rhyme in the 3rd line and a punch line at the end. We're glancing at a limerick because it's such a good example of "frequent rhyme" contributing well to the comedy, plus that ending "payoff line" for which we'll always strive.

Search for limericks on the internet and you'll crack up more than once, I promise. Besides being funny, they're a great lesson in choosing words that flow along nicely in unmistakable rhythm.

While rhyming isn't difficult, it certainly requires care. **Keep your rhymes as natural as possible**, generally resembling the stressed sounds that occur in speech. No lyric should have to be uttered in a really strange, forced way in order to accomplish a rhyme.

Always retain logic, wit, intelligence and good sense when you're creating rhymes. Many beginning songwriters will force a rhyme at the expense of serving the intended message of the lyrics. ("I just wrote 'fennel' there because I needed a rhyme for 'kennel.'" Yikes.)

You can use your own ideas and practice the skills presented in this chapter before moving on, or not. Many opportunities to settle down and apply are coming later. As long as everything seems clear, go ahead and obey your urge for instant gratification. Charge on to Chapter 3.

3

She Loves You, Yeah, Yeah, Yeah

Using Repetition Effectively

All well written songs feature purposeful repetition. Remember in the previous chapter, how we began two different 4-line sections with the same phrase? In doing so, we emphasized a point: *this is what the song is about.*

The catchy word or phrase we keep reminding the audience to remember is the "lyrical hook" – the one thing we want them to recall, if nothing else. It's usually the title of the song. If it isn't, it might as well be, because listeners will perceive it that way!

I'm going to show you how to position this repetitive thing at tried-and-true places in a song. Knowing and applying this info will:

1. Strengthen your comic lyrics in general
2. Anchor and focus them
3. Make them more memorable and professional

Exciting? Yes.

Title Position I – First Line of a Section

This means making the song title line 1 of a 4-line section.

First we'll always make sure we know what we're about; let's create some working specs:

SPECS

Idea: I dislike it when my mom puts me on restriction.
Who's singing: A 9-year old who is grounded
Reason for the song: The singer complains to the world about his/her evil captor.
Working title: "My Mom Won't Let Me Go Out"
Rhyme scheme: ABCB

Naturally we need a supply of words that are relevant to the subject, to work with as fuel for rhymes, so let's throw that together.

General Word Bank

Restricted	Mother	(No) Fun	Girls
Grounded	Captured	Witch	Mean
Free	Date	Protective	Escape

Word Bank Rhymes

Restricted: conflicted, depicted, predicted, convicted, contradicted
Grounded: pounded, impounded, sounded, resounded, founded, hounded
Free: me, key, fee, DDT, employee, Simon Legree, flea, agree, disagree, forty-three
Mother: other, smother, another, brother
Captured: enraptured
Date: mate, rate, late, innate, irate, state, berate
(No) Fun: done, run, gun, pun, son, sun, shun, outdone, outrun
Witch: ditch, bitch, rich, itch, hitch, glitch, pitch
Protective: invective, elective, corrective, collective, defective, detective, directive
Girls: pearls, squirrels, unfurls, hurls, swirls, twirls, curls
Mean: seen, queen, wean, intervene, seventeen, Halloween, ball peen
Escape: rape, scrape, tape, grape, ape

Want to give it a go? I've selected possible "B" rhymes for you, below:

My mom won't let me go out   A
_____grounded   B
_____   C
_____impounded   B

My mom won't let me go out
_____ free
_____
_____ Simon Legree

My turn:

My mom won't let me go out
It's Friday and I'm grounded
She's the cop and I'm the Chevy
Locked up and impounded

My mom won't let me go out
Lordy, I wants to be free
She apparently thinks it's the pre-war south
And she's Missus Simon Legree

Can you see how the common phrase at the beginning of each section serves to tie the two together, keep us on the subject, and suggest that this is the title of the song?

We can keep the ABCB rhyme scheme and accomplish that same effect another way – read on.

Title Position II – Last Line of a Section

This time we're going to place the title at the end of multiple 4-line sections. It will be our crowning phrase.

Setting up the 4th line to rhyme is a different sort of challenge, and we'll create an additional, new kind of word bank to prepare for the game. We'll call it **"Title Rhymes for 'end of the title.'"**

(It becomes important to create a title that isn't too hard to rhyme – not "Keep Your Filthy Paws Off My *April*.")

Here goes with a new idea:

SPECS

Idea: I dislike people who never return favors or hospitality.
Who's singing: The person complaining about this
Reason for the song: The singer tells the offender that the "friend-ship" is over.
Working title: "Friends Like You I Don't Need"
Rhyme Scheme: ABCB

General Word Bank
(To assist with relevant vocabulary in the lyrics)

Ungrateful	Reciprocate	Uncool	Dinner
Favor	Invite	Pal	Inconsiderate
Hospitality	Borrow	Buddy	Exclude
Help out	Money	Social	
Treat	Remember	Party	
Pick up the tab	Lunch	Birthday	

Word Bank Rhymes
(We don't urgently require any because we're only planning to rhyme the title.)

Title Rhymes for "Need"
Speed, read, plead, feed, bead, weed, heed, impede, steed, freed, concede, bleed, creed, deed, indeed, precede, proceed, lead, steed

There. Now we're armed for battle. Why not try completing some lyrics before you read my "answers?" Relax and let the title give you ideas for how to lead up to it in the 4th line. I've chosen "B" rhyme set-ups as possibilities.

How to approach this? Think about line 4, to which everything will lead…see if you can compose something (anything!) for line 2 based on that last word in the line, below.

…*I feel the need for* **speed**…*Why must you always* **speed***?*… *Goodbye, so long, God***speed**…*Guess I'm just not your* **speed**… after that you'll continue to look at the "puzzle," browse the general word bank and listen for possibilities in your head, to fill in the remaining blank lines.

1. _____

2. _____ speed

3. _____

4. Friends like you I don't need

1. _____

2. _____plead

3. _____

4. Friends like you I don't need

I wrote this...

You never invite me to parties
Guess I'm just not your speed
But you always call when you're horny
Friends like you I don't need

You never come through with a favor
Even when I coax and plead
Why don't you walk west 'til your hat floats?
Friends like you I don't need

Let's do it again with another title and employ another rhyme scheme, just to prove we can.

Idea: I appreciate (like) waitresses.
Who's singing: A classic, career waitress, or several! For comic purposes I would want the singer(s) to be crusty and surly.
Reason for the song: We encourage others to tip.
Working title: "Tip the Waitress, Please"
Rhyme scheme: ABAB

General Word Bank

Diner	Counter	Greeting	Dawn
Coffee	Customer	Food	Early
Java	Tired	Grub	Rush
Denny's	Smile	Jerk	Grill
Late night	24-hour	Stiff(ed)	Burger
Buck	Feet hurt	Stew	Flirt

Word Bank Rhymes

(We need these again because we're rhyming more than just the title line)

Diner: miner, liner, whiner, shiner, Shriner, Four-Oh-Niner, finer, signer
Coffee: toffee, ticked off-y, Hoffy (sausage/ hot dog/ bacon brand name)

Java: guava, lava, baklava

Denny's: "bennies" (Benzedrine), pennies, Jennies, many's

Late night: hate night, late flight, straight white, mate fight

Buck: luck, tuck, stuck, puck, muck, Huck, schmuck, f*ck, suck, duck, pluck

Counter: encounter, discounter, discount 'er, mount 'er

Customer: accustom 'er

Tired: acquired, mired, fired, wired, sired, hired

Smile: dial, bile, awhile, rile, style, tile, file, Kyle, Nile, aisle, isle, pile, mile

24-hour: scrub and scour, need to shower, no wallflower, super power, thunder shower

Feet hurt: neat shirt, sweet flirt

Greeting: meeting, fleeting, competing, beating, heating

Food: nude, prude, lewd, rude, skewed, pooh-poohed, 'tude (attitude), shooed, mood

Grub: bub, shrub, cub, nub, tub, hub, pub, stub, snub

Jerk: work, perk, clerk, Turk, shirk, Dirk, Kirk, lurk

Stiff: whiff, tiff, riff, jiff' (Stiffed: lift, sift, rift, miffed)

Stew: cue, blue, do, shrew, few, I.Q., new, woo, too, two, brew

Dawn: Shawn, lawn, Goldie Hawn, fawn, pawn

Early: squirrel-y, pearly, whirly, surly, curly, hurly-burly, girlie

Rush: hush, blush, "shush," mush

Grill: still, nil, quill, pill, mill, until, frill, skill, fill, kill

Burger: (No rhymes, but it might come in handy.)

Flirt: curt, pert, inert, hurt, shirt, squirt, quirt, dirt, spurt, blurt

Title Rhymes for "Please"

Sneeze, wheeze, knees, sees, Belize, freeze, frees, seize, Pleiades, tease, appease, carrots and peas, squeeze, breeze, iced teas, fleas, bees, trapeze, fees, "jeez," Chinese, Japanese

Reminders from Mission Control

Be open to inspiration from the title in order to create a lyric story that concludes in line 4.

I've suggested rhyme set-ups in line 2 of both "puzzles" below – don't let the blank space in lines 1 and 3 freak you out! Proceed this way...

First theorize something for line 2. Next, imagine what line 1 could be, leading into line 2.

Line 3 will probably be the most challenging to make work – it has to rhyme with Line 1, to accomplish the ABAB rhyme scheme. We can do it!

1. _____ (rhyme set-up for line 3)   A

2. _____ knees   B

3. _____ (rhyme fulfillment of line 1)   A

4. Tip the waitress, please   B

1. _____

2. _____ iced teas

3. _____

4. Tip the waitress, please

For each section I made up line 2 first, and then ended up writing this:

> *She fetches grub for a lotta schmucks*
> *It's murder on the knees*
> *The late night crowd at Denny's sucks*
> *Tip the waitress, please*
>
> *If you camp at the counter from ten 'til two*
> *And drink sixteen iced teas*
> *Leave no doubt about your I.Q.*
> *Tip the waitress, please*

Again observe the overall effect – repeating the title in line 4 serves to marry the sections nicely. The audience recalls "Tip the Waitress, Please" as the inevitable title, and the lyrics stay on track.

At this point I want to introduce you to some helpful definitions that have everything to do with *what is purposefully repeated in the lyrics to a song.*

A **thematic line** is one that we choose to repeat regularly, just as we've been doing. It becomes the theme of a song by virtue of its recurrence. The rest of the lyrics support it, support it, and support it.

If a thematic line keeps recurring at the end of a section, it's called a **tag line** or a **refrain**. (You've heard this term in non-musical English – *"'Did you get me some Wild Turkey?'* was her constant refrain.")

A **chorus**, on the other hand, is its own special "section" of a song, containing more than a single line. We hear a chorus come around at least twice, maybe 3 or more times, and it WILL contain the thematic line. The length and content of a chorus can vary; read on...

Now that we've established the terms in the preceding box, let's talk about choruses in more detail.

Title Position III – In the Chorus

We'll consider a chorus to consist of either 2 or 4 lines of lyrics. Examples:

1. TWO-LINE CHORUS

a. We can state the title, then simply repeat it.
> *My favorite thing to do is nothin' at all*
> *(Oh,) My favorite thing to do is nothin' at all*

b. We can state the title, then vary it in the second line.
> *My favorite thing to do is nothin' at all*
> *Nothin', nothin' at all*

c. We can set up the title to rhyme, then state it.
> *In the winter and spring, summer and fall,*
> *My favorite thing to do is nothin' at all*

d. We can do exactly what we just did in example c, except that we'll change the rhyme set-up each time the chorus occurs. Don't panic, examples follow; first we have to set up a word bank...

Title Rhymes for "All"

Gall, ball, tall, fall, wall, haul, brawl, call, stall, crawl

50

Now it's easy to create something like the examples below, for any number of choruses:

> *If you ever need an able hand, please don't **call***
> *My favorite thing to do is nothin' at **all***

> *When I'm sittin' on my butt, I'm havin' a **ball***
> *My favorite thing to do is nothin' at **all***

That's it for 2-line choruses. I mention them to be complete; however, when we create entire sets of lyrics later on, we'll always make our choruses 4 lines long, as these are the most common.

2. FOUR-LINE CHORUS

The simplest version of this consists of taking 2 lines of lyrics and echoing them, making a total of 4:

> *My favorite thing to do is nothin' at all*
> *Oh, my favorite thing to do is nothin' at all ("Everybody!")*
> *My favorite thing to do is nothin' at all*
> *Oh, my favorite thing to do is nothin' at all*

Now, here's a possible 4-line combo in which we repeat the title a few times, then throw in a new line 3, setting up the title to rhyme at the end:

> *My favorite thing to do is nothin' at all*
> *Oh, my favorite thing to do is nothin' at all*
> ***If you ever need an able hand, please don't call***
> *My favorite thing to do is nothin' at all*

You can also write regular 4-line sections and simply **conclude each time with the title**. In this case we'd likely make the rhyme scheme of the choruses different than those of the verses.

Here's one last possibility you should be aware of:

When the words you're imagining are set to music, some "notes" might be chosen to be held longer, so that all the "2-line" chorus lyrics we've looked at previously could become 4 musical lines instead.

Examine the following examples, in which I've decided to suggest that the lyrics occupy 4 lines instead of 2. We're imagining that it takes longer to sing each line:

> *My favorite thing to do --*
> *Is nothin'--- at all*
> *(Oh,) my favorite thing to do --*
> *Is nothin'--- at all*

Get the idea? Check out the rest of these examples...

> *In the winter and the spring--*
> *Summer --- and fall ---*
> *My favorite thing to do ---*
> *Is nothin' --- at all*

If you ever need an able hand --
Please -- don't call --
My favorite thing to do ---
Is nothin' --- at all

When I'm sittin' on my butt --
I'm havin' -- a ball ---
My favorite thing to do ---
Is nothin' --- at all

Finally, know that not all songs feature a chorus. If we state a thematic line at the beginnings or ends of other sections in a song, that's sufficient repetition. We don't need a chorus.

Title Position IV – End of the Song

We can always choose to state the title as the very last line of a song even if we haven't been putting it at the ends of previous sections. (It's an option; sometimes you'll prefer a "surprise line" at the end – one that the audience hasn't heard before – to provoke a final laugh.)

Realize the following:

1. When your song has a chorus, the title is already built into its conclusion! And as you'll see when we create entire sets of lyrics in Chapter 4, a song that includes a chorus will be inclined to end with a chorus.

2. If you've already been ending multiple sections of a song with the title, this is very convenient. Just do it again at the end.

3. If you've been beginning multiple sections of a song with the title, no problem — when it's time, simply adjust the rhyme scheme to create a special, ending section with the title also placed at the end.

We are now on a downhill run to creating funny lyrics for complete songs! I suggest a delicious meal, a nap, a shower and an energy drink. Then meet me at Chapter 4.

Take Me Back to the Bridge

Understanding the Components

You know how to write a 4-line section; at this point I'm going to introduce you to the traditional ways we can define such sections as building blocks of a larger product.

Once we've taken a good look at the following, "usual, sectional components" of songs, it will be easy to create and arrange them in various ways.

No need to memorize the info in 1-4, below... just relax, focus and read through each explanation and example.   Return for later reference when you like.

1. The Verse

A verse is like a chapter in a story. It commonly has 4 lines and features a rhyme scheme. All songs contain some number of verses.

We've written many 4-line sections so far that could be considered verses. We began or ended each of those sections with a thematic line.

Now let's add a third possibility...verses that contain NO thematic line:

Verse 1   *When I was just a normal guy*
                My sense of fashion was rough
                No layers of frilly and slinky and sheer
                Jeans and a T were enough

Verse 2   *One pair of shoes was plenty*
                'Til these thoughts began to hatch
                Of Manolo Blahniks with five-inch heels
                And evening bags to match

In the verses above we haven't yet included a thematic line in the song...we would need to do so later, in a chorus.

2. The Chorus

You learned how to create a chorus in Chapter 3. Remember, when a song contains a chorus, our thematic line will be in there, so we don't need to put it in the verses. Here's an example of a chorus that could follow the two verses in #1:

> *Now I watch my pennies*
> ***It's expensive to be a transvestite***
> *I'm through with Payless tennies*
> ***It's expensive to be a transvestite***

The chorus above would recur in the song, and we'd probably vary the first and third lines with new rhyming words, each time it comes around.

3. The Bridge

James Brown made "Take me back to the bridge" a famous utterance, introducing a musical term to millions who still have no idea what it is.

A bridge typically has 4 lines, just like a verse.

The words of a bridge can be an obvious detour – a place to reflect alternatively on the lyric story in progress, as if to say "on the other hand," or "what I really mean is..."

The words to a bridge don't change the subject of the song, but they often elaborate from a different perspective, like the past or future. In a song that tells a funny story, the bridge might be some significant "turning point" in the story.

It can have the same rhyme scheme as the song's verses do, or a different one. Usually its lyrics do not state the title of the song. Musically, it will have its own distinctive melody. (Many songs feature a bridge; many don't. It's not compulsory.)

Check out this example of a bridge that could come along during our song in progress:

> *It's not that I long to be female*
> *Don't want that set of specs*
> *This Rocky Horror thing is fun*
> *But I'll keep my Johnson and pecs*

Do you see that it's a kind of digression, but we're still securely on the subject? A bridge is the perfect place to express yourself in this way. It's very common for a song to have a single bridge, and two are quite possible.

4. The Tag

Finally, there's an optional, rather theatrical section at our disposal called a tag. We sometimes create one as a unique ending for a song. A tag is like a caboose – something a little different, just to wrap things up in a fun way. Lyrically it might be 4 lines; maybe more. It may have a different rhyme scheme than we've heard previously in the song.

Here's a theoretical tag for "It's Expensive to be a Transvestite:"

> *So if you wanna get into drag---*
> *You better get your hands on some swag---*
> *It's spicy--- but it's pricey,*
> *To be a transvestite------------*

In this "P. S." to the rest of the lyrics, I've employed an AABC rhyme scheme; there's an internal rhyme in line 3, and the last line doesn't rhyme with anything. Sometimes I finish a tag with the song title, sometimes not.

In the next two chapters we'll construct entire sets of lyrics, using combinations of the sections we've just defined: verses, bridges, choruses and tags...song after song about transvestites. I'M KIDDING. Go to Chapter 5.

5

Lyric Games People Play

How to Build the Lyrics of Entire Songs

READY, SET

As I promised, time now to assemble our sections (verses, choruses, bridges, tags) in a number of traditional ways, creating lyrics to entire songs.

These various constructions are called **song forms**. Song forms can be labeled with letters, similar to the way we identified rhyme schemes. For instance:

> "Verse / Verse / Verse" would be AAA.
> "Verse / Verse / Bridge / Verse" would be AABA.
> "Verse / Verse / Chorus" would be AAB.

GO

In parts 1-6 to follow, we'll trade off working with a set of parameters. First I'll create a set of funny lyrics based on those parameters, and you can look carefully at what I did. Then it will be your turn to give it a try with a different song idea. This should be a blast. Please don't take it too seriously – just use our tools and procedures and have some fun.

The upcoming "lyric puzzles" are shown in a workbook style to make clear how to proceed, but of course it won't be practical to write in the book… you need paper, pencils and eventually a rhyming dictionary – or – you can do everything on a word processing screen, and even search for rhymes on the web.

Slow down, take it easy with this big chapter. Peruse the whole thing and enjoy it. Then, when you decide it's a good time to actually start doing the work, do not hurry. If you try to do too much too fast, you'll get fried and exhausted and throw this book at the wall.

Give yourself at least a day or two between each assignment – you need brand new, fresh energy for each one. It's also a great idea to work for awhile on a single set of lyrics, then come back a day later for a second look…you'll have unexpected, better ideas.

LYRIC EXAMPLE 1 Something I Dislike

SPECS

Idea: Job interviews
Who's singing: Someone who dislikes job interviews
Reason for the song: We hear what the job applicant is thinking during an interview.
Working title: "Doin' the Interview Song and Dance"
Song form: Verse/Verse/Verse (AAA)
Rhyme scheme: ABCB
Title position: The 1st line of each verse

General Word Bank

Job	Impression	Attitude	Sweat
On time	Gig	Classified	Situation
Nervous	Smile	Jitters	Late
Talk	Ad	(Un)employed	Relax
Money	Pay	Tension	Fired
Lie	Hope	Position	Impress
Discussion	Power	Boss	Brag

Word Bank Rhymes

Job: rob, bob, snob, fob, hob nob, lob

On time: lime, nickel-and-dime, slime, sublime, crime, I'm, paradigm, climb, chime

Nervous: service, serve us, disservice

Talk: walk, chalk, hawk, stalk, squawk

Money: honey, sunny, sonny, funny, bunny, runny, "pun-ny," "Attila the Hun-y"

Lie: fly, why, sigh, tie, suit and tie, pry, guy, oh my, apply, die, "to die," try, fry

Discussion: percussion, Russian, concussion, repercussion

Impression: digression, intercession, recession, freshen, session, depression, confession, repossession

Gig: pig, dig, trig(onometry), "cig," fig, jig, wig, renege, prig, big, bigwig

Smile: file, mile, awhile, dial, pile, style, denial, beguile

Ad: sad, mad, dad, "rad," fad, tad, egad, had, cad, pad, glad

Pay: stay, may, at bay, lay, sauté, flambé, play, hooray, okay, beret, say, pray, way, day, toupee

Hope: mope, pope, elope, dope, cope, soap, rope

Power: sour, scour, cower, flower, deflower, tower, shower, hour, flour

Attitude: latitude, gratitude, "combat-itude"

Classified: pacified, "sass-ified"

Jitters: litters, fence sitters, baby sitters, critters, bitters, hitters, twitters, no-hitters, transmitters, glitters, embitters

(Un)employed: enjoyed, overjoyed, annoyed

Tension: pension, abstention, mention, condescension, apprehension, convention

Position: sedition, suspicion, volition, acquisition, mission, rendition, ignition, dishin'

Boss: floss, emboss, cross, sauce, across, gloss, toss, moss

Sweat: met, bet, debt, cigarette, pet, fret, martinet, castanet, net, get, let, upset

Situation: equation, inflation, vacation, stagnation, fixation, application, sensation, dedication, connotation, collaboration, indication, organization, prevarication, elation

Late: wait, bait, state, berate, great, plate, fate, weight, overweight, sedate, overstate

Relax: sax, to the max, wax, hacks, fax, stacks, tax, cracks, packs

Fired: hired, wired, sired, expired, acquired, tired, retired, aspired, admired, required

Impress: more or less, confess, digress, mess, largesse, finesse, Wes (you never know, this could be handy), dress, caress, distress, obsess, possess, guess, second-guess, Porgy and Bess

Brag: stag, rag, drag, hag, nag, flag, bag, tag, lag, snag, gag, swag

EXAMPLE

"Doin' the Interview Song and Dance"

Verse 1   *Doin' the interview song and dance*
It's this or pilfer and rob
Why can't I just have a trust fund?
I don't really have time for a job

Verse 2   *Doin' the interview song and dance*
That's quite the cologne, I must say
If those are your kids, I'm sorry
… I just realized that's a toupee

Verse 3   *Doin' the interview song and dance*
Startin' to sweat like a pig
Before I fry in this suit and tie
Just gimme the goddamn gig

I put an internal rhyme in the 3rd line of the last verse – this isn't essential at all, but it's nice for the conclusion and is always an option. (If you do this in the first verse, do it in all of them.)

LYRIC PUZZLE **1** Something I Dislike

SPECS

Idea: Getting up early
Who's singing: Someone who dislikes getting up early
Reason for the song: The singer justifies his habit of sleeping in.
Working title: "I Have to Get My Beauty Sleep"
Song form: Verse/Verse/Verse (AAA)
Rhyme scheme: ABCB
Title position: The lst line of each verse

General Word Bank

Rest	Night	Get up	Mattress
Rejuvenation	Morning	Rise	Pillow
Noon	Late	Shine	Quiet
Forty winks	Wake	Snore	Disturb
Bed	Yawn	Sun	Lazy
Slumber	Coffee	Hibernate	No calls
Attractive	Toast	Spring	Pretty

Word Bank Rhymes

Rest: crest, best, zest, lest, pest, fest, guest, behest, jest, nest, arrest, infest, test, distressed, breast, quest

Rejuvenation: stipulation, situation, manifestation, elation, complication, libation, coronation, sedation, sensation, vacation, vocation, celebration, deprivation, expectation

Noon: soon, swoon, tune, balloon, moon, buffoon, prune, loon, goon, raccoon

Forty winks: stinks, sphinx, links, blinks, sinks, finks, jinx, thinks, slinks

Bed: red, read, head, said, instead, dead, Ned, lead, wed, bread, dread, spread, fed, fled, pled

Slumber: number, outnumber, lumber, encumber (looser: mumbler, stumbler, bumbler, fumbler, tumbler)

Attractive: reactive, active, hyperactive, retroactive, refractive, distractive

Night: bright, light, delight, fright, sight, tight, polite, impolite, unite, uptight, black and white, slight, Snow White, plight, kite

Morning: adorning, warning, "popcorn-ing," mourning, scorning

Late: date, equate, freight, mate, state, bait, Kate, rate, wait, estate, deflate, abate, create, weight, straight, fate, hate

Wake: lake, stake, bake, make, quake, Jake, cake, steak, break, ache, partake, flake

Yawn: gone, brawn, prawn, come on, faun/fawn, carry on, pawn, drawn, head on

Coffee: toffee, Hoffy (sausage/hot dog/bacon brand name), ticked off-y

Toast: roast, most, ghost, host, coast, post, boast, almost

Get UP: pup, schtup, cup, met up, set up, sup, yup, step up

Rise: prize, surprise, surmise, unties, cries, goodbyes, dies, tries, fries, lies, pies, sighs, wise, comprise, advise, disguise, despise, devise, size

Shine: wine, dine, fine, line, mine, pine, sign, vine, divine, decline, design, in line, online

Snore: bore, whore, core, door, more, for, tore, shore, pour, pore, lore, store, roar, floor

Sun: done, fun, hon', gun, nun, stun, won, ton, bun, shun, well done, twenty-one, one

Hibernate: (loose – second rate, make me late, irritate, exacerbate)

Spring: fling, ring, bling, sing, king, Bing, zing, Ming, ding, swing, thing, string, ka-ching, a la King, wing, cling

Mattress: (loose – status, apparatus, gratis, actress)

Pillow: billow, willow, armadillo, peccadillo, cigarillo

Quiet: diet, try it, buy it, tie it, dye it, riot, fry it, deny it

Disturb: blurb, curb, 'burb, Herb, herb, Serb, perturb, verb, superb

Lazy: hazy, Patrick Swayze, lazy, daisy, glaze-y, mayonnaise-y

No calls: Joe calls, some 'ho calls, Godot calls, H. Ross Perot calls, Brigette Bardot calls, faux calls, snowfalls

Pretty: kitty, pity, ditty, shitty, titty, city, nitty-gritty, committee, witty, Walter Mitty

"I Have to Get My Beauty Sleep"

Verse 1   (Title)_____   A
           _____   B
           _____   C
           _____   B

Verse 2   (Title)_____   A
           _____   B
           _____   C
           _____   B

Verse 3   (Title)_____   A
           _____   B
           _____   C
           _____   B

LYRIC EXAMPLE 2 — Something I Dislike

Idea: People who constantly borrow small amounts of money

Who's singing: Someone who constantly borrows small amounts of money

Reason for the song: We satirize behavior by putting the song in the voice of the offender.

Working title: "Dude, Can You Front Me Five Big Ones?"

Song form: Verse/Verse/Verse (AAA)

Rhyme scheme: ABCB

Title position: The lst line of each verse

General Word Bank

Broke	Buck	Annoying	Quit(s)
Sponge	Loan	Irritating	Over it
Weasel	Lend	Predictable	No more
Deadbeat	Bum	Old	Done
Loser	Payback	Stop	Need
Cash	Repay	Rob	Wallet
Money	Greenback	Cease	Credit

Word Bank Rhymes

Broke: bloke, smoke, Coke, folk, toke, stoke, poke, baroque, okey-doke, joke

Sponge: lunge, expunge, grunge, plunge

Weasel: diesel, easel, measle, a squeeze'll, cheese'll, expertise'll, the Japanese'll

Deadbeat: dead meat, red meat, instead meet, bed sheet, head to feet, head to the suite

Loser: cruiser, schmoozer, snoozer, boozer, peruser (peruse 'er, etc....), excuser, accuser, user, chooser, muser, diffuser, abuser, confuser, infuser (loose – Hoosier)

Cash: mash, bash, stash, hash, clash, panache, lash, rash, '62 Nash, Ogden Nash, flash

Money: honey, bunny, sunny, runny, punny, sonny

Buck: muck, cluck, duck, suck, tuck, stuck, truck, f*ck, luck, puck, Huck

Loan: bone, flown, phone, groan, hone, shown, moan, condone, Eva Peron, tone, cone, stone, drone, known, crone, Tyrone, throne, blown

Lend: fend, addend, send, friend, mend, amend, bend, extend, tend, trend, apprehend

Bum: scum, dumb, succumb, yum, plum(b), ho-hum, rum, drum, strum, mum, come

Payback: stay back, way back, day pack, haystack, Ray-O-Vac, display rack, Hey Jack, laid back (loose – maniac, meglomaniac)

Repay: flambé, touché, Jose, beret, ballet, away, today, enchante, delay, Santa Fe, passé, filet, croquet, bouquet, okay (loose – lemonade, Dennis Quaid, afraid, parade, blockade)

Greenback: get my/your – routine back, hygiene back, tambourine back, magazine back

Annoying: enjoying, employing, toying, cloying, callboy-ing, playboy-ing

Irritating: irrigating (loose – titillating, instigating, I'm still waiting)

Predictable: evictable (loose – transmittable, committable, (in)hospitable)

Old: sold, bold, cold, rolled, mold, (un)told, fold, gold, hold, cajoled, polled, paroled

Stop: sop, top, pop, hop, mop, strop, flop, prop, cop, crop, drop, chop, atop

Rob: sob, knob, snob, bob, cob, fob, lob, mob, no prob', throb, swab, gob, glob

Cease: police, grease, peace, niece, fleece, crease, lease, apiece, increase, release, valise

Quits: sits, kits, mitts, zits, tits, knits, pits, spritz, on the fritz, bits, ditz, hits, The Ritz

Over it: (loose – go for it)

No more: what for, galore, to the core, I'm sore, there's the door, out the door, on the floor, furthermore, bore, whore, more, store, Ecuador, implore, explore, tore

Done: run, bun, 'hon, shun, stun, fun, gun, Attila the Hun, pun, nun, ton, won, sun, son

Need: speed, deed, concede, impede, proceed, weed, freed, lead, bead, feed, plead, read

Wallet: call it, stall it, scrawl it, recall it, haul it

Credit: edit, fed it, said it, embed it, read it, spread it, get it, let it, fret it, bet it, regret it, upset it

EXAMPLE 2

"Dude, Can You Front Me Five Big Ones?"

Verse 1   *Dude, can you front me five big ones?*
I caught that subtle groan
But it ain't like I need a hundred
And we're talkin' short-term loan

Verse 2   *Dude, can you front me five big ones?*
I'm just momentarily broke
Friends should be there for each other
Like last year when I bought you that Coke

Verse 3   *Dude, can you front me five big ones?*
Come on now, don't be sore
I found a buck on your bathroom floor
So here's one, and I'll owe ya four

Quite by accident I found a place for an additional rhyme when I was writing the 3rd verse, and therefore made the rhyme scheme ABBB. This is not exactly a tag (see page 58), but a "bonus rhyme" in the final section is a pleasing touch.

LYRIC PUZZLE 2 Something I Dislike

Idea: Telemarketers
Who's singing: A telemarketer
Reason for the song: We satirize the institution of telemarketing in its own voice.
Working title: "Hello, How Are You This Evening?"
Song form: Verse/Verse/Verse (AAA)
Rhyme scheme: ABCB
Title position: The 1st line of each verse

General Word Bank

Deal	Today	Best	Good
Call	Buy	Time	Happy
Chosen	Price	Phone	Trust
Receive	Bargain	Shop	Easy
Zip Code	Visa	True	Cheaper
Offer	Now	Surrender	Safe
Special	Quickly	Authorize	Plan

Word Bank Rhymes

Deal: steal, meal, real, reel, feel, squeal, peel, peal, appeal, repeal, heel, heal, congeal

Call: stall, fall, ball, mall, maul, all, brawl, crawl, haul, wall, tall

Chosen: frozen, dozin', hosin', posin', (loose – jones-in')

Receive: believe, conceive, deceive, reprieve, perceive, weave, leave, Steve, peeve, heave, bereave, "The Beav,'" achieve, grieve, sleeve, eve

Zip Code: quip-mode, Crip code, shipload

Offer: coffer, scoffer, cougher

Special: flesh'll, a creche'll, Bangladesh'll

Today: say, pray, nay, lay, okay, beret, fray, touché, play, may, hooray, pay

Buy: my, try, why, cry, pie, hi, dry, guy, lie, sigh, tie, die, pry

Price: nice, twice, thrice, dice, lice, entice, vice, vise, ice, rice, suffice, device, advice

Bargain: jargon

Visa: he's a, "freez-uh," degrees o' (uh), "Ebenez-uh," Leaning Tower of Pisa

Now: how, cow, frau, wow, pow, sow, bow, the Dow (loose – mouth, south, cowed, prowl, scowl, proud, howl, foul, fowl, jowl, towel, frown, town, renown, sound, found)

Quickly: prickly, sickly, slickly, "partic'ly"

Best: nest, rest, behest, fest, jest, guest, test, breast, lest, pest, quest, west, zest, depressed, impressed, distressed, obsessed, possessed, pressed

Time: chime, dime, I'm, mime, slime, prime, lime, crime, grime, time, climb, sublime

Phone: bone, shown, blown, cone, condone, hone, sewn/sown, flown, loan, prone, zone

Shop: pop, stop, strop, mop, bop, cop, drop, fop, hop, prop, sop, chop, flop, swap

True: coup, sue, Sioux, blue, new, anew, few, drew, coo, Kung Fu, loo, woo, do, stew, moo, who, grew, Jew, boo-hoo, through, too, taboo, screw, black and blue, brew

Surrender: lender, spender, blender, apprehend/comprehend 'er, sender, tender, fender

Authorize: (loose – cauterize, sodomize, patronize, fraternize, win a prize)

Good: should, could, wood, would, hood, stood

Happy: crappy, sappy, pappy, nappy, yappy, toe-tappy, in your lappy, scrappy

Trust: bust, cussed, dust, just, lust, fussed, bussed, must, rust, nonplussed (loose – us)

Easy: breezy, sleazy, queasy, sneezy, tease-y, pretty-pleas-ey, cheesy

Cheaper: deeper, reaper, keeper, beeper, leaper, steeper, creeper, peeper, sweeper

Safe: chafe, waif

Plan: man, ban, can, fan, Iran, clan, Ku Klux Klan, pan, Stan, tan, van (loose – stand, land, panned, manned, fanned, canned, tanned, banned, band, sand, demand

"Hello, How Are You This Evening?"

Verse 1 (Title)_____ A
        _____ B
        _____ C
        _____ B

Verse 2 (Title)_____ A
        _____ B
        _____ C
        _____ B

Verse 3 (Title)_____ A
        _____ B
        _____ C
        _____ B

LYRIC EXAMPLE **3** Personal Predicament

SPECS

Idea: I don't understand cars.

Who's singing: Someone who doesn't understand cars

Reason for the song: The singer confesses his plight to a mechanic, hoping not to be ripped off.

Working title: "I Don't Know a Piston from an Overhead Cam"

Song form: Verse/Verse/Bridge/Verse   (AABA)

Rhyme scheme: Verses – ABAB   Bridge – AABB

Title position: Refrain – the 4th line of each verse (see page 49)

General Word Bank

Automobile	Car	Fix (it)	Transmission
Dirty	Hood	Go	Pray
Authority	Nuts and bolts	Repair	Beseech
Know-how	Dipstick	Mystery	Naïve
Skill	Fear	Drive	Help
Mechanic	Dummy	Wrench	Travel
Garage	Understand	Rattle	Tune up

Word Bank Rhymes

Automobile: conceal, reveal, spiel, we'll, he'll, ideal, kneel, steal, zeal, squeal, meal

Dirty: flirty, thirty (loose – sturdy, wordy, birdie, Princess "Fergie," hurdy gurdy)

Authority: sorority, majority, minority, priority, seniority, superiority

Know-how: snowplow, go now, "whoa, now"

Skill: pill, bill, shrill, kill, nil, skill, still, 'til, quill, fill, hill, Jack and Jill, dill, mill

Mechanic: panic, manic, Germanic, organic, satanic, volcanic, titanic, Hispanic, messianic (loose – frantic, pedantic, romantic)

Garage: mirage, barrage, collage, "gar-bahjz," montage, corsage

Car: star, bar, tar, far, afar, jar, ajar, mar, par, Baba Yar, har-de-har-har

Hood: could, should, would, wood, stood, good

Nuts and bolts: dolts, molts, Eric Stolz, volts, colts, jolts

Dipstick: lipstick, cryptic, nitpick (loose – Bisquick, filmstrip, quick fix)

Fear: gear, hear, rear, dear, steer, cheer, career, jeer, peer, queer, tear, veer, we're, brassiere, adhere, appear, disappear, clear, severe, perservere, pioneer, Mouseketeer, racketeer, sheer, sphere, beer, interfere, sincere, insincere, chandelier, cashier

Dummy: gummy, rummy, mummy, tummy, rum-tum-tummy, crummy, yummy

Understand: stand, land, panned, manned, fanned, canned, tanned, banned, band, sand, Ku-Klux-Klanned, demand

Fix it: nix it, mix it, eighty-six it, kicks it, flicks it, depicts it, restricts it

Go: bow, foe, hoe, Joe, low, mo', no, po', status quo, Godot, H. Ross Perot, Brigitte Bardot, sew, sow, tow, row, to and fro', apropos, stow, flow, glow

Repair: affair, bear, bare, au contrare, declare, debonair, midair, millionaire, stare, air, care, square, pair, rare, fair, fare, dare, hair, hare, lair, mare, prayer, impair, heir, wear, snare

Mystery: history, blistery, transistor-y, brother and sister-y

Drive: hive, deprive, live, alive, strive, arrive, derive, Clive

Wrench: bench, wench, stench, trench, drench, French, mensch, clench

Rattle: battle, embattle, cattle, chattel, prattle, tattle

Transmission: volition, suspicion, admission, addition, ambition, ignition, optician

Pray: say, bay, decay, olé, flambé, hooray, okay, day, today, lay, may, nay, tray, oy vey, Beaujolais

Beseech: beach, peach, leech, speech, screech, teach, preach, breach

Naïve: receive, reprieve, believe, conceive, bereave, eve, Steve, leave, weave, sleeve, achieve, deceive, perceive, Tel Aviv, "The Beav'"

Help: yelp, kelp, whelp

Travel: unravel, gavel, gravel

Tune up: festoon up, balloon up, raccoon pup

Title Rhymes for "Cam"

Wham, bam (thank you) ma'am, cram, dram, gram, ham, jam, Sam, Uncle Sam, Pam, "sha-zam," clam, am, gam, lam, scram, yam, exam, goddamn, Trans Am, Grand Am, dam, damn, Hoover Dam, Madame, slam, tram, "BLAM," scam, sham, lamb, ram

"I Don't Know a Piston from an Overhead Cam"

Verse 1   *Sir, I come humbly to your house of repair*
Something is amiss with my old Trans Am
We made it to your door on a fume and a prayer
And I don't know a piston from an overhead cam

Verse 2   *You can see by my outfit that I'm not a millionaire*
Today you are a lion, while I am but a lamb
I appeal to your ethics as I stand and declare
That I don't know a piston from an overhead cam

Bridge   *Daddy was a tyrant; demanding and severe*
"Oil my boots before I slap ya! Go fetch another beer!"
I had to wax the squad car; I kept it looking good
But he never let me see beneath the hood

Verse 3   *To gaze into your eyes is to know that you care*
And would never stoop to perpetrate a scam
On this soul laid bare, hoping you will treat him fair
Tho' he don't know a piston from an overhead cam

The length of the title has affected the length of theses lines, making each one longer than the ones in lyric examples 1 and 2. Also notice that I slightly varied the title line each time, to accommodate what preceded it. It's always fine to do that as long as you retain the gist.

I threw an internal rhyme (bare/fair) into line 3 of the last verse as a variation, to make the ending a little fancier. At the end I abandoned grammar ("treat him fair, tho' he don't know...") because I thought it contributed to the comedy.

LYRIC PUZZLE **3** Personal Predicament

SPECS

Idea: I'm a chain smoker.

Who's singing: A chain smoker

Reason for the song: The singer explains why smoking a cigarette is necessary at every waking moment.

Working title: "That's When I Have Another Cigarette"

Song form: Verse/Verse/Bridge/Verse (AABA)

Rhyme scheme: Verses – ABAB   Bridge – AABB

Title position: Refrain – the 4th line of each verse

General Word Bank

Nicotine	Stress	Smoke	Smoker
Friend	Nervous	Light up	Matches
Addiction	Drink	Drag	Stop
Relief	Beer	Happy	Cessation
Jittery	Caffeine	Meal	Content
Smell	Social	Phone	Chill
Odor	Out of Control	Step outside	Take a hit

Word Bank Rhymes

Nicotine: trick a teen, (loose – in-between, friggin' mean, kick The Queen, quick 'n' lean, thick 'n' green, lick a Marine, Mister Clean, Ben Vereen, ever seen)

Friend: send, bend, mend, tend, amend, lend, extend, blend, attend, depend, dead end

Addiction: friction, depiction, fiction, restriction, affliction, eviction, conviction

Relief: beef, grief, belief, disbelief, chief, brief, debrief, aperitif

Jittery: glittery, skittery, quitter-y, littery, twittery

Smell: hell, bell, tell, fell, mademoiselle, sell, show and tell, rebel, farewell, yell, spell, compel, well, wishing well, excel, dwell, clientele, cell, infidel, hotel, motel

Odor: decoder, loader, boater, floater, middle-of-the-roader, explode 'er, freeloader

Stress: mess, less, caress, excess, largesse, press, express, digress, duress, success

Nervous: service, serve us, disservice

Drink: blink, sink, link, mink, pink, shrink, brink, clink, kink, zinc, fink

Beer: near, fear, clear, steer, hear, career, queer, tear, veer, year, peer, rear, gear

Caffeine: bean, mean, seen, lean, between, queen, Ben Vereen, clean, keen, teen, wean, careen, ball peen, canteen, beguine, marine, thirteen, dry clean, machine, scene

Social: No rhymes here, but the word seems valuable.

Out of control: coal, dole, mole, hole, pole, on a roll, toll, stole, cajole, goal

Smoke: joke, Coke, okey-doke, bloke, poke, woke, broke, stoke, stroke, spoke, soak

Light up: pup, sup, cup, schtup, "wassup," what up, "ten-hup," pre-nup (loose – erupt, disrupt, interrupt)

Drag: bag, sag, hag, nag, lag, gag, jag, wag, fag, stag, flag

Happy: sappy, pappy, crappy, toe-tappy, nappy, scrappy

Meal: deal, seal, feel, real, surreal, peel, peal, steel, steal, zeal, even keel, kneel

Phone: bone, scone, hone, moan, loan, condone, alone, sown, sewn, tone, stone, cologne

Step outside: bride, hide, guide, sighed, confide, lied, tied, wide, (in)side, stride, pride

Smoker: joker, soaker, toker, poker, woke 'er, stoker, choker, broker

Matches: latches, snatches, batches, patches, catches, attaches, hatches

Stop: pop, top, bop, cop, hop, hip hop, shop, crop, fop, mop, prop

Cessation: elation, equation, celebration, nation, constipation, gyration, automation, vacation, vocation, altercation, alteration, masturbation, orientation, sensation

Content: lament, bent, sent, rent, lent, dent, gent, tent, vent, went, Kent, extent

Chill: pill, frill, dill, kill, mill, nil, sill, quill, still, hill, drill, until, will, bill, chill

Take a hit: bit, kit, flit, mitt, shit, twit, wit, quit, admit, permit, knit, lit, pit, writ, zit

Title Rhymes for "Cigarette"

Bet, get, debt, met, let, pet, set, vet, wet, regret, Annette, Gillette, fret, barrette, minuet, martinet, roulette, heavy set, launderette, dudette, bassinet, castanet, majorette, vignette, crepe suzette, statuette, vinaigrette, upset, quintet, quartet, duet, baguette, beget, net, jet, eau de toilette, sweat, abet, whet, threat, Collette, gazette, briquette, novelette, silhouette

"That's When I Have Another Cigarette"

Verse 1   _____   A
             _____   B
             _____   A
             (Title)_____   B

Verse 2   _____   A
             _____   B
             _____   A
             (Title)_____   B

Bridge*   _____   A
             _____   A
             _____   B
             _____   B

Verse 3   _____   A
             _____   B
             _____   A
             (Title)_____   B

* Remember: We typically leave the title out of a bridge. Shift perspective on the subject in this section.

LYRIC EXAMPLE **4** Personal Wish

SPECS

Idea: I wish I could just hit people who make me mad.

Who's singing: The person who has this wish

Reason for the Song: The singer shares a mildly perverse fantasy. (Wouldn't it be funny if the character performing the song were a little old lady, or some other milquetoast-y, unlikely person? As I mentioned at the end of Chapter 1, always visualize some "ideal singer" of a funny song; it will inspire you.)

Working title: "I Wish I Could Smack Anybody I Want"

Song form: Verse/Verse/Bridge/Verse (AABA)

Rhyme scheme: Verses – ABCB   Bridge – AABB

Title position: The 1st line of each verse

General Word Bank

Mad	Whack 'em	Smarty	Teach 'em
Slap	Mouth	Sass	Nice
Kisser	Thump	Lip	Mean
Slug	Boss	Fight	Rude
Punch	Show 'em	Scrappy	(Un)kind
Nose	Pissed	Surprise	Scared
What-for	Piss me off	Last straw	Look out

Word Bank Rhymes

Mad: sad, dad, "rad," had, bad, glad, cad, tad, clad, grad, lad

Slap: crap, trap, sap, tap, whap, zap, clap, lap, wrap, rap, flap, nap, yap, snap

Kisser: diss 'er, miss 'er, pisser, hisser (loose – sister, resist 'er)

Slug: mug, bug, hug, dug, jug, smug, tug, rug, pug, lug

Punch: brunch, scrunch, lunch, hunch, crunch

Nose: suppose, hose, pose, rose, impose, propose, toes, snows, bows, close, expose, foes, knows, goes, sews, so-and-sos, prose, beaux, rows, bro's

What-for: door, score, floor, more, pour, whore, shore, ignore, implore, gore

Whack 'em: sack e'm, track 'em, crack 'em, stack 'em, hijack 'em, hack 'em

Mouth: south

Thump: stump, dump, rump, pump, clump, ump', bump, frump

Boss: loss, sauce, moss, floss (loose – cost, lost, exhaust, tossed)

Show 'em: grow 'em, know 'em, snow 'em, throw 'em, bestow 'em, blow 'em

Pissed: resist, mist, kissed, list, tryst, dismissed, hissed, "dissed," insist, persist, enlist, exist, untwist, assist, grist, fist

Piss me off: cough, trough, scoff (loose - soft, loft)

Smarty: hearty, Havarti, ex parte, commedia del arte, arty (loose – tardy)

Sass: brass, ass, crass, pass, bass, Mama Cass, lass, mass (loose: fast, last, cast…)

Lip: nip, hip, sip, tip, pip, Crip, blip, whip, ship, trip, drip, flip, quip, zip, dip, gyp, snip, equip, skip, strip, grip, chip, clip

Fight: right, tight, bite, white, light, might, night, quite, site, cite, height, flight

Scrappy: happy, pappy, crappy, nappy, sappy, snappy

Surprise: surmise, flies, ties, unties, pies, goodbyes, lies, dies, wise, tries, disguise, guise, fries, eyes, demise, despise, devise, revise, advise, size, sighs

Last straw: paw, flaw, draw, saw, claw, gnaw, hee-haw, jaw, maw, law

Teach 'em: reach 'em, beach 'em, beseech 'em, bleach 'em

Nice: twice, rice, spice, lice, mice, price, dice, vise, vice, Heidi Fleiss, entice

Mean: between, seen, teen, keen, marine, routine, lean, bean, clean, magazine

Rude: dude, nude, prude, exude, food, mood, include, exclude, 'tude, shrewd, intrude

(Un)kind: combined, signed, consigned, blind, mined, mind, shined, behind, bind, lined, maligned, fined, refined, pined, wind, wined and dined

Scared: cared, shared, compared, dared, prepared, bared, stared, fared, repaired

Look out: pout, snout, trout, lout, about, route, scout, shout, doubt, sprout, clout, bout, kraut, gout, grout, stout

EXAMPLE **4**

"I Wish I Could Smack Anybody I Want"

Verse 1   *I wish I could smack anybody I want*
I'm tired of being "dissed"
It's just about time to kick some ass
And let people know I'm pissed

Verse 2   *I wish I could smack anybody I want*
I get way too much lip
The occasional one-two punch would do it
And off I would merrily skip

Bridge   *It's not that I'm so scrappy*
But it would make me happy
To have the option of bruising some snout
Whenever I'm out and about

Verse 3   *I wish I could smack anybody I want*
Deliver a nice surprise
To the next rude dude with attitude
Right between the eyes

Note the triple, internal rhyme in line 3 of verse 3. This peps up the conclusion.

LYRIC PUZZLE **4** Personal Wish

SPECS

Idea: I wish my boyfriend were quieter.

Who's singing: Someone who wishes her/his boyfriend would talk less

Reason for the song: The singer shares the problem with us as a warning. (There's room for affection here, i.e., "but he's really a great guy.")

Working title: "Gregorio Can Be a Little Chatty"

Song form: Verse/Verse/Bridge/Verse (AABA)

Rhyme scheme: Verses – ABCB   Bridge – AABB

Title position: The 1st line of each verse

General Word Bank

Quiet	Torrent	Edgewise	Eternal
Shut up	Flood	Interruption	Never ending
Nip it	Gush	Interject	Interjection
Pie hole	Yap	Incessant	Digression
Mouth	Share	Thoughts	Go on
Gab	Sharing	Yak	Elaborate
Talky	Loud	Say	Verbal

Word Bank Rhymes

Quiet: diet, riot, tie it, try it, buy it, cry it, dye it, fry it

Shut up: pup, sup, cup, schtup, what up, "ten-hup," pre-nup (loose – erupt, disrupt, interrupt)

Nip it: snippet, whippet, flip it, grip it, sip it, tip it, whip it, dip it, lip it, trip it

Pie hole: dry hole, eye hole, my hole, some shy hole,

Mouth: south

Gab: drab, "fab," tap, blab, crap, jab, cab, nab, lab, flab, scab, slab, stab, smack-dab

Talky: squawky, gawky

Torrent: abhorrent, warrant

Flood: bud, Scud, pud, (stick in the) mud, dud, Elmer Fudd, HUD, crud, stud, spud, blood, thud

Gush: lush, hush, shush, plush, rush, flush, mush, slush, brush, thrush

Yap: lap, cap, rap, slap, snap, gap, nap, map, pap, flap, crap, tap, whap, zap

Share: scare, bare, hair, hare, care, dare, debonair, tear, declare, fare, fair, lair, mare, affair, pair, wear, flare, flair, glare, square, spare, rare, forswear, there, air, au pair

Sharing: baring, caring, daring, declaring, faring, pairing, wearing, glaring, sparing

Loud: shroud, wowed, cowed, House of Saud, proud, endowed, chowed, allowed, crowd, holier-than-thou'd, plowed, cow-towed (loose – found, sound, pound, round...)

Edgewise: pledge-wise

Interruption: corruption, disruption, eruption (loose – gumption)

Interject: sect, protect, erect, (dis)infect, disinfect, decked, flecked, (hen)pecked, (in)direct, project, elect, effect, affect, detect, collect, (dis)connect, reject, expect, inspect, select, interject, resurrect, subject, respect, recollect (loose – wreck, check, neck, exec, spec, speck, heck...)

Incessant: depressant, fluorescent, iridescent, luminescent, adolescent, effervescent

Thought: bought, caught, naught, taught, brought, ought, distraught, fought, wrought

Yak: back, flak, sack, track, tack, jack, lack, black, whack, smack, crack, hack, knack

Say: bray, day, today, hooray, sway, okay, fray, dismay, way, away, bay, hey, hay, beret, nay, bourre, flambé, oi vey, stay, stray, tray, pray, gray, pay, gay, may, pray, spray, filet

Eternal: internal, infernal, nocturnal, kernel, maternal, paternal, fraternal, external

Never ending: bending, sending, extending, attending, blending, tending, apprehending, comprehending, ascending, descending, appending, mending, pending

Interjection: ejection, erection, projection, protection, election, genuflection, section, C-section, reflection, affection, (mis)direction, convection, detection

Digression: session, Hessian, depression, digression, freshen, concession, confession, suppression, oppression, succession, regression, expression, obsession, agression

Go on: con, baton, filet mignon, (for)gone, lawn, Goldie Hawn, faun, fawn, Sorbonne, yon, "Hey Mon," thereupon, Don Juan, ex-con, brawn, drawn

Elaborate: (loose – exacerbate, masturbate, irritate, vacillate, encapsulate, gravitate)

Verbal: herbal, gerbil

"Gregorio Can Be a Little Chatty"

Verse 1   (Title)_____   A
           _____   B
           _____   C
           _____   B

Verse 2   (Title)_____   A
           _____   B
           _____   C
           _____   B

Bridge   _____   A
           _____   A
           _____   B
           _____   B

Verse 3   (Title)_____   A
           _____   B
           _____   C
           _____   B

LYRIC EXAMPLE 5 State a Problem

SPECS

Idea: I have an intrusive neighbor.

Who's singing: The neighbor who is always imposing himself on my life

Reason for the song: We satirize behavior by putting the song in the voice of the offender.

Working title: "Bye for Now, But I'll Catch You Later!"

Song form: Verse/Verse/Bridge/Verse (AABA)

Rhyme scheme: Verses – ABCB   Bridge – AABA

Title position: Refrain - the 4th line of each verse

General Word Bank

Neighbor	Occupied	Wait	Borrow
Buddy	Oblivious	Hey	Needy
What's up	Ignore me	Hey there	Get a life
Busy	Second	Hi	Check in
Impose	Minute	Howdy	Call
Intrude	Butt in	See ya	Knock
Pry	Inquire	Favor	Barge

Word Bank Rhymes

Neighbor: saber, (be)labor

Buddy: muddy, study, bloody, cruddy, fuddy duddy

What's up: pup, sup, cup, schtup, what up, "ten-hup," pre-nup (loose – erupt, disrupt, interrupt)

Busy: tizzy, Tin Lizzy, fizzy, dizzy, frizzy, is he (?)

Impose: close, nose, suppose, pose, toes, so-and-sos, blows, knows, froze, hose, woes, doze, chose, goes, close, oppose, propose, (de)compose, clothes, rose, disclose

Intrude dude, nude, prude, exude, food, mood, include, exclude, 'tude, shrewd, rude

Pry: goodbye, why, try, high, sigh, fry, Dubai, fly, cry, pie, River Kwai, lie, my, nigh, to die, rye, wry, ply, sly, by, nearby, passer by, shy, guy, hi, aye, dry

Occupied: no rhymes here, other than the unlikely "I KNOCKED, he lied."

Oblivious: lascivious

Ignore me: adore me, floor me, implore me, bore me, explore me, deplore me, front-

85

door me, reform me, inform me, hard-core me

Second: beckoned, (mis)reckoned

Minute: in it, spin it, pin it, "agin' it," win it, begin it

Butt in: kin, tin, spin, pin, win, begin, sin, grin, din, shin, violin, chagrin, gin, thin, twin, been, chin

Inquire: wire, hire, fire, conspire, dire, The Shire, choir, mire, tire, liar, lyre, pyre, squire, inspire, expire, flyer

Wait: plate, abate, bait, crate, date, fate, gate, hate, mate, late, (in)state, innate, equate, berate, rate, first-rate, cut-rate, create, debate, freight, grate, great, skate, trait, elate (a)wait, weight, straight

Hey: bray, day, today, hooray, sway, okay, fray, dismay, way, away, bay, hay, beret, nay, bourre, flambé, oi vey, stay, stray, tray, pray, gray, pay, gay, may

Hey there: stay there, okay there, lay there, stray there

Hi: fly, why, sigh, my, (de)cry, (un)tie, shy, belie, try, fry, die, goodbye, awry, dry, pie

Howdy: dowdy, rowdy, Saudi, cloudy, (magna or summa) cum laude (loose – pout-y, mouthy, southie)

See ya: idea, sangria, tortilla, bougainvillea, panacea, pizzeria, diarrhea, Ave Maria, guarantee ya, free ya, iced-tea ya, DDT ya

Favor: savor, (time) saver, Lifesaver, waiver, paver, quaver, raver, flavor, shaver, flag waver, craver

Borrow: sorrow, tomorrow, claro, Charro

Needy: beady, seedy, yes-indeedy, greedy, speedy, tweedy (loose – graffiti, meaty, sweetie, tweety, sleety, (en)treaty, ziti)

Get a life: knife, wife, strife, fife, Barney Fife

Check in: Could be useful…see "butt in" above for "in" rhymes

Call: haul, maul, squall, fall, gall, hall, tall, Robert Duvall, shawl, crawl, stall, wall

Knock: crock, sock, flock, stock, cock, dock, block, hock, jock, mock, (un)lock, wok

Barge: (en)large, Marge, "sarge," (dis)charge

Title Rhymes for "Later"

Equator, 'tater, date 'er, gator, crater, hater, waiter, cater, skater, traitor, debater, "the-AY-ter" (theater), creator (looser accent-wise but still okay – dictator, operator, vibrator, spectator, carburetor, perpetrator, violator, generator, appreciate 'er, elevator, flatulator, imitator, liberator, masturbator, replicator, deliberator, defibrillator, exasperator, procrastinator, communicator, devastator)

EXAMPLE 5

"Bye for Now, But I'll Catch You Later!"

Verse 1   *Hey good buddy, what's crackin'?*
Sun's up – don'cha be a couch "pertater!"
Just checkin' in for a quick howdy-do
Bye for now, but I'll catch you later!

Verse 2   *Yoo-hoo, it's just yours truly…*
Guess what, I got a new carburetor!
The buggy's runnin' great, and I thought you'd like to know
Bye for now, but I'll catch you later!

Bridge   *When I come a-knockin', to say "how ya been?"*
You know you got a neighbor who's just like kin!
The guy who used to live here didn't stay very long
And made me feel like I was buttin' in!

Verse 3   *"Buenas Tortillas," mi amigo!*
Sure smells good – you should cater!
Lemme grab a bite and I'll be on my way
Bye for now, but I'll catch you later!

LYRIC PUZZLE 5 State a Problem

SPECS

Idea: Airplane food is bad.

Who's singing: A flight attendant

Reason for the song: We satirize a situation by putting the song in the voice of its representative.

Working title: "Thanks So Much for Dining on United!"

Song form: Verse/Verse/Bridge/Verse (AABA)

Rhyme scheme: Verses – ABCB Bridge – AABA

Title position: Refrain – the 4th line of each verse

General Word Bank

Stale	Fare	Chef	Platter
Dry	Cuisine	Beverage	Plate
Bland	Exquisite	Spork	Plastic
Assembly line	More	Helping	Steam
Taste	Lunch	Gourmet	Hunger
Bad	Dinner	Appetite	Bite
Dessert	Supper	Starving	Swallow

Word Bank Rhymes

Stale: male, mail, bail, bale, kale, Dale, flail, pail, gale, tale, tail, wail, whale, sale, pale

Dry: goodbye, why, try, high, sigh, fry, Dubai, fly, cry, pie, River Kwai, lie, my, nigh, to die, rye, wry, pry, ply, sly, by, nearby, passer by, shy, guy, hi, aye

Bland: sand, band, banned, land, hand, stand, understand, planned, fanned, tanned, canned, manned, panned

Assembly line: a tremble-y dine

Taste: haste, waste, waist, erased, laced, paced, faced, aced, raced, based, baste, chaste, debased, encased, misplaced, replaced

Bad: pad, dad, had, sad, glad, mad, tad, plaid, shad, "rad," cad, ad, egad, fad, clad, Chad

Dessert: squirt, dirt, inert, pert, alert, curt, shirt, flirt, hurt, Kurt, assert, avert, subvert

Fare: scare, bare, hair, hare, care, dare, debonair, tear, declare, fair, lair, La Mer, affair, pair, wear, flare, flair, glare, square, spare, rare, forswear, there, air, au pair

Cuisine: gasoline, between, queen, keen, teen, seen, mean, benzene, Murine, scene, Celine, dean, clean, ball peen, gene, lean, bean, magazine, green, sixteen, convene, chlorine, caffeine, Saltine, routine, lean, pristine, machine, dry clean, spleen, marine

Exquisite: what is it (?), (re)visit, quiz it, show-biz it

More: score, door, floor, bore, core, whore, galore, tore, wore, yore, for, fore (!), lore, store, boar, drawer, gore

Lunch: brunch, crunch, scrunch, punch, hunch, munch

Dinner: skinner, winner, sinner, inner, grinner, thinner, spinner, beginner

Supper: fix 'er upper, scupper, cupper, shoot 'em upper

Chef: Jeff, deaf, clef, Steph' (loose – left, bereft, heft, deft)

Beverage: leverage

Spork: torque, Bjork, cork, dork, stork, Mork (and Mindy), fork, pork

Helping: yelping

Gourmet: sorbet, okay, array, hooray, stay, may, fey, play, ray, stray, today, flambé, say, hey, hay, Jay, bay, nay, way, away, day, spray, clay, pay, tray

Appetite: schmappetite (sorry), map it right, cap it tight

Starving: carving

Platter: spatter, clatter, matter, Mad Hatter, batter, patter, latter, fatter, chatter (loose – ladder, bladder, madder, sadder, gladder, "badder,")

Plate: bait, wait, date, late, hate, berate, elate, ate, fate, trait, pate, crate, freight, rate

Plastic: spastic, fantastic, bombastic, elastic, drastic, monastic, sarcastic, scholastic, gymnastic, orgiastic, enthusiastic, dynastic (loose – classic, Jurassic)

Steam: deem, cream, seem, seam, beam, team, ream, (self-) esteem, dream

Hunger: younger, Felix Unger

Bite: tight, right, all right, white, night, kite, sight, flight, light, bright, quite, slight, height, indict, excite, plight, trite, sprite, incite, delight, recite, blight, ignite

Swallow: hollow, follow, wallow, Apollo

Title Rhymes for "United"

Delighted, lighted, (un)requited, farsighted, nearsighted, excited, (be) knighted, ignited, slighted, blighted, indicted, righted, recited, expedited, overnight-ed, copyrighted, dynamited, highlighted, incited, Coked and Sprite-ed*

*I've been liberal here with stressed-sound matches on this list, because there is a shortage of rhymes for "United." These are pretty good though; I think you'll be fine.

"Thanks So Much for Dining on United"

Verse 1   _____   A
                _____   B
                _____   C
                (Title)_____   B

Verse 2   _____   A
                _____   B
                _____   C
                (Title)_____   B

Bridge   _____   A
                _____   A
                _____   B
                _____   A

Verse 3   _____   A
                _____   B
                _____   C
                (Title)_____   B

LYRIC EXAMPLE 6   Something I Like

SPECS

Idea: Spicy food

Who's singing: The person who likes spicy food

Reason for the song: Jubilation. It's just a happy, "three cheers for X" song.

Working title: "It's Sweet When You Crank Up the Heat"

Song form: Verse/Verse/Bridge /Verse; Bridge /Verse   (AABA; BA)

Rhyme scheme: Verses – ABCB   Bridges – ABCC

Title position: Refrain – the 4th line of each verse

General Word Bank

Hot	Combust	Kung Pao	Yum
Yummy	Burn	Combustion	Spicy
Mean	Infernal	Tongue	Delight
Fire	Ferocious	Mouth	Like
Fiery	Pepper	Consume	Cayenne
Caliente	Jalapeno	Extinguish	Aggressive
Potent	Chile	Flame	Tasty

Word Bank Rhymes

Hot: shot, tot, not, pot, lot, slot, dot, cot, knot, sot, twat, yacht, squat, gavotte, forgot, got, plot, Anwar Sadat

Yummy: gummy, rummy, mummy, tummy, rum-tum-tummy, crummy, dummy

Mean: gasoline, between, queen, keen, teen, seen, benzene, Murine, scene, Celine, dean, clean, ball peen, gene, lean, bean, magazine, green, sixteen, convene, chlorine, caffeine, saltine, routine, lean, pristine, machine, dry clean, spleen, marine, cuisine

Fire: hire, wire, sire, expire, acquire, tire, retire, aspire, admire, require

Fiery: diary, priory

Caliente: al dente, cognoscente, exactamente

Potent: (loose – rodent)

Combust: cussed, just, rust, thrust, lust, (en)trust, mistrust, must, dust, discussed, gust, mussed, nonplussed, bussed, crust, fussed

Burn: urn, (over)turn, Vern, concern, learn, fern, earn, churn, stern, yearn, adjourn, discern, nocturne, sauternes

Infernal: eternal, vernal, kernel, journal

Ferocious: atrocious, precocious, supercalifragilisticexpialidocious (loose – hypnosis, halitosis, neurosis, osmosis, psychosis, roaches, Nacogdoches)

Pepper: leper, stepper, schlepper, prepper, prep 'er

Jalapeno: (loose – volcano, Drano)

Chili: Billy, dilly, filly, silly, shrilly, lily, frilly, Milli Vanilli, willy-nilly

Kung Pao: how, cow, frau, wow, now, sow, bow, the Dow (loose – mouth, south, cowed, prowl, scowl, proud, howl, foul, fowl, jowl, towel, frown, town, renown, sound, found)

Combustion: (loose – Russian, Prussian, concussion, percussion, repercussion, discussion)

Tongue: rung, wrung, (un)sung, hung, dung, lung, "brung," young, stung, (un)strung, far-flung, sprung, among

Mouth: south

Consume: bloom, (en)tomb, Khartoum, room, boom, whom, doom, "'shroom," (nom de) plume, flume, assume, resume, gloom, groom, fume, consume, zoom, vroom, loom, broom

Extinguish: distinguish (loose – English, "tingle-ish," Kris Kringle-ish)

Flame: tame, (over)came, same, game, maim, lame, shame, aim, frame, acclaim, disclaim, exclaim, (re)claim, name, blame

Yum: dumb, plum, plumb, hum, rum, glum, from, tum, (dim) sum, (over)come, become, succumb, mum, numb, strum, bum, slum, alum, swum, crumb, "crum," some, thumb, drum, ho-hum

Spicy: dicey, pricey, icy

Delight: bite, tight, right, all right, white, night, kite, sight, flight, light, bright, quite, slight, height, indict, excite, plight, trite, sprite, incite, recite, blight, ignite

Like: tyke, "trike," bike, hike, Mike, psych, dike, dyke, spike, pike

Cayenne: glen, then, when, hen, pen, Zen, den, wren, again, Big Ben, julienne, amen, comedienne, doyenne

Aggressive: progressive, possessive, excessive, depressive, oppressive, expressive, impressive, digressive, successive, obsessive

Tasty: hasty, pasty

Title Rhymes for "Heat"

("Sweet" is of course in the title…) eat, beat, complete, fleet, elite, meat, neat, repeat, replete, cheat, meet, (en)treat, conceit, discreet, aquavit, Marguerite, retreat, defeat, feet, (back)seat, street, upbeat, deceit, tweet, DEET, Crete, bleat, feet, delete

EXAMPLE 6

"It's Sweet When You Crank Up the Heat"

Verse 1
Combustible cuisine
That's what I love to eat
Ca-li-en-te? Exactamente!
It's sweet when you crank up the heat

Verse 2
Fire inside my food
Makes a meal complete
I say "Wow" when the Kung goes Pao!
It's sweet when you crank up the heat

Bridge 1
Brie and crackers are elegant
But just a little boring
I'd rather write in my journal
Of something more infernal

Verse 3
Give me ferocious fare
Serve up an aggressive treat
Throw in cayenne and I'll say "Amen"
It's sweet when you crank up the heat

Bridge 2
Save your timid dishes
For when I'm a hundred and two
Before I purchase a plot
I'll keep gobblin' up what's hot

Verse 4
Lay on the peppers, please
Give 'em a front row seat
I wanna ignite with every bite
It's sweet when you crank up the heat

Here we have lyrics that are more cute and clever than "funny," per se. This kind of material will work beautifully for a performer's crazy characterization (a la Carmen Miranda? You get the picture…), and the end product thus becomes hilarious.

LYRIC PUZZLE 6 Something I Like

SPECS

Idea: Dating a lot of different people at once
Who's singing: The person who likes to date a lot of different people at once
Reason for the song: The singer justifies his/her romantic way of life.
Working title: "Playin' the Field is My Style"
Song form: Verse/Verse/Bridge /Verse; Bridge /Verse (AABA; BA)
Rhyme scheme: Verses – ABCB   Bridges – ABCC
Title position: Refrain – the 4th line of each verse

General Word Bank

Promiscuous	Easy	Week	Rendezvous
Dating	Share	Month	Pick up
Fun	Casual	Year	Go out
Commit	Commitment	Night	Sex
Marry	Wink	Hitched	Stable
Lark	Flirt	Engagement	Attraction
Hooked	Movie	Fling	Serious

Word Bank Rhymes

Promiscuous: loose – conspicuous, ambiguous…looser – discus, viscous, hibiscus…we could even make up words like "frisk-uous"

Dating: (in)stating, (be)rating, equating, abating, baiting, skating, gold-plating

Fun: pun, stun, run, hon', (un)done, bun, honeybun, sun, ton, Attila the Hun, gun, spun, shun, won, begun, well-done, twenty-one, one-on-one

Commit: bit, chit, lit, split, kit, shit, fit, "git," hit, tit, wit, zit, mitt, knit, quit, grit, pit, snit, spit, legit, to whit, submit, obit, omit, Sanskrit, slit

Marry: tarry, berry, ferry, fairy, (mis)carry, contrary, parry, Larry, sherry, wary, Glengarry, prairie, hari-kari, Stradivari, Tom, Dick and Harry, nary, airy

Lark: stark, dark, park, quark, "narc," hark, shark, bark, Cutty Sark, ark, arc, mark

Hooked: booked, cooked, looked,

Easy: sleazy, wheezy, Parcheesi, sneezy, disease-y, cheesy, queasy, greasy,

Share: scare, bare, hair, hare, care, dare, debonair, tear, declare, fare, fair, lair, mare,

affair, pair, wear, flare, flair, glare, square, spare, rare, forswear, there, air, au pair
Casual: loose – irascible, passable
Commitment: remitment
Wink: plink, zinc, link, stink, kink, mink, fink, pink, sink, clink
Flirt: curt, pert, inert, hurt, shirt, squirt, quirt, dirt, spurt, blurt
Movie: groovy
Week: sneak, cheek, tweak, leak, sheik, freak, meek, sleek, creek, bleak, reek, wreak, unique, Monique, boutique, squeak, creak, Greek
Month: no rhymes
Year: leer, peer, steer, mere, we're, fear, queer, tear, beer, Al Wazir, nadir, brassiere, chandelier, gear, seer, overseer, clear, dear, (over)hear, jeer, ear, near
Night: bright, light, delight, fright, sight, tight, polite, impolite, unite, uptight, black and white, slight, Snow White, plight, kite
Hitched: stitched, bewitched, ditched, pitched, itched, bitched, enriched
Engagement: "enragement"
Fling: sling, "bling," ring, ding, sting, king, string, zing, ping, Ming, wing, bring, spring, cling, Bing, sing, wring, thing
Rendezvous: "Genghis Khan-dezvous," "john-devous," "Wrath of Khan-devous"
Pick up: stick up, lick up, hick up, nick up, prick up, slick up, sick pup
Go out: pout, snout, trout, lout, about, route, scout, shout, doubt, sprout, clout, bout, kraut, gout, grout, stout
Sex: ex, hex, Oedipus Rex, checks, Czechs, decks, wrecks, flecks, Tex, perplex, necks, specks, specs, execs, Erma Bombeck's, collects, (dis) infects, dissects, reflects, protects, corrects, directs, pecs, pecks, hunts and pecks, neglects, objects, suspects, selects, connects
Stable: cable, table, Betty Grable, fable, gable, (dis)able, Cain and Abel, enable, Mabel, sable, label, a babe'll
Attraction: faction, (counter)action, traction, putrefaction, distraction, satisfaction, subtraction, reaction
Serious: delirious, imperious, mysterious, Sirius

Title Rhymes for "Style"

Dial, bile, awhile, rile, style, tile, file, Kyle, Nile, aisle, isle, pile, revile, smile, denial, (be)guile, I'll, compile, trial, defile, (worth)while, awhile, vile, vial (looser accent-wise – mistrial, juvenile, crocodile, pedophile, infantile, versatile, profile)

"Playin' the Field is My Style"

Verse 1 _____ A
        _____ B
        _____ C
        (Title)_____ B

Verse 2 _____ A
        _____ B
        _____ C
        (Title)_____ B

Bridge 1 _____ A
        _____ B
        _____ C
        _____ C

Verse 3 _____ A
        _____ B
        _____ C
        (Title)_____ B

Bridge 2 _____ A
        _____ B
        _____ C
        _____ C

Verse 4 _____ A
        _____ B
        _____ C
        (Title)_____ B

6

Fasten Seatbelt, Tray Table Up

You Supply the Song Ideas

How's it going so far? It's important for you to complete the work in Chapter 5 before proceeding with this one. If you want more practice, I recommend that you take advantage of the ideas and word banks for **Lyrics Examples 1-6** and write alternative lyrics to my own.

You're ready to move ahead? Great. Time for you to take on a larger creative role – in this chapter I'll continue to provide examples and some of the specs in the lyric puzzles, while you handle their actual song ideas. We will also add to the picture by working with some lyrics that include choruses and tags. I hope you're having fun. Turn the page.

LYRIC EXAMPLE **7** Unlikely Situation

SPECS

Idea: A used car salesman who is a gospel preacher on the side
Who's singing: The used car salesman
Reason for the song: The singer preaches the gospel as only a used car salesman can.
Working title: "You Oughta Take Jesus for a Test Drive"
Song form: Verse/Verse/Bridge /Verse; Bridge /Verse (AABA; BA)
Rhyme scheme: Verses – ABCB   Bridges – ABCB
Title position: The 1st line of each verse

General Word Bank

Keys	Guarantee	Satan	Bank
Ignition	Comfortable	Satanic	Prayer
Bucket seats	Speed	Pride	Heal
Fuel injection	Size	Blue Book	Saves
Power	Price	Money	Sin(s)
Style	Luxurious	Acceleration	Faith
Mileage	Heaven	Affordable	Forgiven
Security	Hell	Rates	Believe
Storage	Insurance	Try	

Word Bank Rhymes

Keys: tease, squeeze, Belize, tweeze, seize, (over)sees, disease, bees, trees, he's/she's, SUVs, knees, reprise, wheeze, jeez, ease, sneeze, breeze, freeze, frees, appease, Pleiades
Ignition: addition, mission, transmission, volition, suspicion, rendition, apparition, extradition, premonition (loose – derision, decision, nuclear fission, collision)
Bucket seats: sweets, cleats, eats, beats, completes, fleets, meats, repeats, cheats, meets, (en)treats, bleats, retreats, defeats, (back)seats, streets, deceits, tweets, Keats
Fuel injection: correction, reflection, election, deflection, infection, section, dissection, detection, complexion, erection, direction, protection
Power: sour, flour, tower, dour, cower, wow 'er, our, (thunder)shower, (de)flower, devour, scour
Style: dial, bile, awhile, rile, tile, file, Kyle, Nile, aisle, isle, pile, revile, smile, denial, (be)guile, I'll, compile, trial, defile, (worth)while, awhile, vile, vial (looser accent-wise – mistrial, juvenile, crocodile, pedophile, infantile, versatile, profile)
Mileage: "smileage"
Security: (im)purity, obscurity, (im)maturity, prematurity, surety

Storage: porridge, forage

Guarantee: (loose – impunity, mediocrity, severity, eternity, alacrity, apparently, transparency, hilarity, temerity, F.T.D., parakeet, verily)

Comfortable: no rhymes

Speed: read, plead, feed, bead, weed, heed, impede, steed, freed, peed, concede, bleed, creed, deed, indeed, precede, proceed, lead, need

Size: prize, surprise, surmise, unties, cries, goodbyes, dies, tries, fries, lies, pies, sighs, wise, comprise, advise, disguise, comprise, despise, devise

Price: spice, lice, mice, thrice, twice, nice, dice, entice, splice, Heidi Fleiss, ice, precise, suffice, rice, vice, vise, device, concise, advice (priced – Christ)

Luxurious: curious, spurious, hurry us

Heaven: seven, eleven, Devon, Andre Previn

Hell: shell, tell sell, bell, mademoiselle, Estelle, rebel, repel, compel, gazelle, (be)fell, gel, quell, smell, spell, well, yell, dispel, hotel, motel, noel, Muscatel, swell, belle

Insurance: occurrence, assurance, deterrents, transference, currents

Satan: baitin', (a)waitin', inflatin', deflatin', hatin', datin' (be)ratin', matin', skatin', creatin', (in)statin', understatin', lady-in-waitin'

Satanic: manic, panic, Germanic, Hispanic, organic, titanic, volcanic, mechanic, messianic

Pride: tide, (be)lied, sighed, side, ride, snide, hide, pride, wide, collide, abide, cried, tried, died, (un)tied, pried, complied, me-oh-my-ed

Blue Book: new book, debut book, true book, Jew book, how-to-book, who's-who-book, boo-hoo book, pooh-pooh book, Winnie the Pooh book, can too cook!

Money: bunny, honey, sunny, sonny, "punny," runny, funny

Acceleration: situation, consternation, aberration, nation, altercation, vacation, elation, invitation, jubilation, equation, libation, station, trepidation, liberation, sensation, abdication, flatulation

Affordable: board-able, horde-able, portable, recordable, awardable

Rates: hates, waits, (in)states, understates, abates, baits, crates, delates, inflates, mates, skates, dates, creates, debates, plates

Try: fry, why, high, sigh, tie, die, lie, fly, guy, my, me-oh-my, pie, pry, sky, rye, nigh

Bank: rank, tank, sank, flank, stank, skank, drank, blank, franc, Hank, "tranq(uilizer)"

Prayer: dare, fair, share, au pair, declare, (for)swear, stare, glare, rare, lair, spare, wear, aware, there, hair, tear, square, flare, flair, stair

Heal: teal, meal, reel, real, feel, squeal, peel, peal, appeal, repeal, heel, heal, congeal, deal

Saves: craves, braves, caves, graves, knaves, paves, raves, waves, behaves, waives, (en)slaves

Sins: fins, pins, bins, grins, shins, wins, spins, skins, begins, violins, twins, inns

Faith: wraith (loose – eighth) With a lisp – grace, place, face, home base, race, case

Forgiven: striven, livin', David Niven, driven

Believe: receive, conceive, deceive, reprieve, perceive, weave, leave, Steve, peeve, heave, bereave, "The Beav," achieve, grieve, sleeve, eve

"You Oughta Take Jesus for a Test Drive"

Verse 1   *You oughta take Jesus for a test drive*
If you're lookin' for a heavenly ride
Once you get a taste of His power and grace
In Him ye shall always abide

Verse 2   *You oughta take Jesus for a test drive*
To pass on this deal would be a sin
I'm on my knees with a set of keys
Prayin' that you'll take Him for a spin

Bridge 1   *The ultimate insurance*
Is His divine protection
When you don't know which way to turn
He'll steer you in the right direction

Verse 3   *You oughta take Jesus for a test drive*
If you want acceleration
Forget the Blue Book and get His new book
It's loaded with inspiration

Bridge 2   *No job, no credit, no problem!*
There's no need to think twice
Brother, keep your cash in the bank
He's already paid the price

Verse 4   *You oughta take Jesus for a test drive*
He's a real low-maintenance guy
And guaranteed for eternity
Believe me, He just won't die

Note that this is a genuine sales spiel from the singer's point of view, not an invalidation of his position. Always remember that you're writing in the voice of the singer and be true to it, even as you exaggerate in order to be funny.

I did an internal rhyme in the third line of each verse, which we've established to be fine but never a requirement. The bridges are written in the same rhyme scheme as the verses, but have no internal rhymes.

LYRIC PUZZLE **7** Unlikely Situation

> **Idea:** _____
>
> **Who's singing:** _____
>
> **Reason for the song:** _____
>
> **SPECS** **Working title:** _____
>
> **Song form:** Verse/Verse/Bridge/Verse; Bridge/Verse (AABA; BA)
>
> **Rhyme scheme:** Verses – ABCB   Bridges – ABCB
>
> **Title position:** The 1st line of each verse

1. Create a General Word Bank.

2. Create a list of Word Bank Rhymes.

"Working Title"

Verse 1   (Title)_____   A
           _____   B
           _____   C
           _____   B

Verse 2   (Title)_____   A
           _____   B
           _____   C
           _____   B

Bridge 1   _____   A
           _____   B
           _____   C
           _____   B

Verse 3   (Title)_____   A
           _____   B
           _____   C
           _____   B

Bridge 2   _____   A
           _____   B
           _____   C
           _____   B

Verse 4   (Title)_____   A
           _____   B
           _____   C
           _____   B

LYRIC EXAMPLE **8** State a Problem

SPECS

Idea: There are too many pretentious people around here.

Who's singing: A pretentious person

Reason for the song: We satirize the problem by putting the song in the voice of the offender.

Working title: "I've Got a Meeting with Some People 'Bout a Thing"

Song form: Verse/Verse/Chorus/Bridge; Chorus/Verse/Chorus (AABC; BAB)

Rhyme scheme: Verses – ABCB, Choruses – ABCC, Bridge – ABCB

Title position: The title concludes each chorus.

General Word Bank

Honcho	Win	Achiever	Image
V.I.P.	Best	Fashion	Fake
Brag	First Place	Trendy	Superficial
Boast	Bucks	Prize	Star
Top	Dash	Big	Façade
One-up	Promotion	Stylish	Bright
Beat	Name Drop	Better	Boor

Word Bank Rhymes

Honcho: poncho, rancho

V.I.P.: free, tea, tee, be, bee, knee, gee, degree, decree, fee, hee-hee, key, me, pee, see, spree, whee, ye, flee, flea, plea, O.D., M.D., O.C.D., yippee, guarantee, gay Paree, do-re-mi

Brag: drag, sag, stag, hag, gag, bag, wag, flag, fag, jag, lag, shag, snag, rag

Boast: most, toast, roast, host, coast, post, almost, ghost

Top: pop, photo-op, shop, lop, crop, stop, hop, hip hop, mop, be bop, cop, drop, slop

One-up: sun up, done up, run up, spun up (loose – runner up)

Beat: heat, sweet, eat, beat, complete, fleet, elite, meat, neat, repeat, replete, cheat, meet, (en)treat, conceit, discreet, aquavit, Marguerite, retreat, defeat, feet, (back)seat, street, upbeat, deceit, tweet, DEET, Crete, bleat

Win: kin, tin, spin, pin, butt in, begin, sin, grin, din, shin, violin, chagrin, gin, thin, twin

Best: nest, rest, behest, fest, jest, guest, test, breast, lest, pest, quest, west, zest, depressed, impressed, distressed, obsessed, possessed, pressed

First place: case, base, debase, face, place, erase, race, trace, mace, pace, grace, disgrace, lace (loose – taste, waste, haste, paste, chaste)

Bucks: ducks, sucks, f*cks, clucks, trucks, plucks, yucks, mucky-mucks, in flux, deluxe

Dash: cash, panache, moustache, crash, bash, hash, stash, mash, brash, rash, lash, splash, thrash

Promotion: locomotion, emotion, Laotian, devotion, potion, lotion, ocean, commotion

Name drop: same cop, lame hop, same shop (loose – bus stop, non-stop, rest stop)

Achiever: (dis)believer, reliever, receiver, weaver, cleaver, beaver, conceiver, fever, griever, deceiver, retriever

Fashion: ashen, ration, (im)passion, compassion, bashin', lashin', stashin', mashin', cashin', trashin', smashin', splashin', thrashin'

Trendy: Wendy, "spendy," modus vivendi

Prize: surprise, surmise, unties, cries, goodbyes, dies, tries, fries, lies, pies, sighs, wise, comprise, advise, disguise, comprise, despise, devise

Big: brig, prig, dig, pig, "cig," rig, "trig," gig, jig, swig, wig, fig, twig

Stylish: beguile-ish, walk-down-the-aisle-ish (looser stresswise – reptile-ish)

Better: sweater, letter, let 'er, debtor, petter, pet 'er, go-getter, get 'er, unfetter, wetter, Irish setter, trend setter, jet setter, cheddar

Image: scrimmage

Fake: lake, take, spake, rake, flake, (a)wake, bake, cake, make, quake, sake, stake, steak, break, brake, snake, shake

Superficial: judicial, interstitial, initial, official, artificial, beneficial, sacrificial

Star: car, tar, far, bar, har-de-har-har, spar, jar, mar, par, Baba Yar, P. R.

Façade: wad, cod, rod, trod, mod, nod, odd, clod, bod, quad, promenade, shod, esplanade, Todd, prod, jihad

Bright: tight, right, all right, white, night, kite, sight, flight, light, quite, slight, height, indict, excite, plight, trite, sprite, incite, delight, recite, blight, ignite

Boor: poor, sure, cure, lure, pure, you're, connoisseur, cocksure, endure, assure, tour, grandeur, entrepreneur, (im)mature, premature, soup du jour, l'amour, Louis L'amour, manure, demure, coiffure, obscure

Title Rhymes for "Thing"

Sling, "bling," ring, ding, sting, king, string, zing, ping, Ming, wing, spring, bring, cling, fling, Bing, swing, sing, wring

EXAMPLE **8**

"I've Got a Meeting with Some People 'Bout a Thing"

Verse 1 *To have a conversation with me is to interrupt*
As I talk about myself non-stop
My feelings, my views, my achievements, my hair
My own is my favorite name to drop

Verse 2 *All day long I am dressed to the nines*
It's my obligation to be trendy
Essential, you see, to give the public what it wants
It's part of my "modus vivendi"

Chorus 1 *I must stay true to my image*
Live up to my own P. R.
Soon I should fly, but I'll give you a ring
I've got a meeting with some people 'bout a thing

Bridge *It's not easy to live with this personal heat*
Where everything must be deluxe
I have to drink vintage, wear vintage, drive vintage
In step with the big mucky-mucks

Chorus 2 *Got a lotta heavy players on my team, dude*
You wouldn't believe who they handle
I can't reveal much, but I'll vaguely sing
I've got a meeting with some people 'bout a thing

Verse 3 *Though I seem so effortlessly, ultimately cool*
Don't envy this glossy facade
I battle the Hollywood powers that be
Indeed, it's my own jihad

Chorus 3 *B'bye, I should go, must motor*
You get this one, and next time — my treat
Just call me Paramount's puppet on a string
I've got a meeting with some people 'bout a thing

LYRIC PUZZLE **8** State a Problem

Idea: _____

Who's singing: _____

Reason for the song: _____

SPECS **Working title:** _____

Song form: Verse/Verse/Chorus/Bridge; Chorus/Verse/Chorus (AABC; BAB)

Rhyme scheme: Verses – ABCB   Choruses – ABCC   Bridge – ABCB

Title position: The title concludes each chorus.

1. Create a General Word Bank.

2. Create a list of Word Bank Rhymes.

3. Create a list of Title Rhymes for _____.

"Working Title"

Verse 1 _____ A
_____ B
_____ C
_____ B

Verse 2 _____ A
_____ B
_____ C
_____ B

Chorus 1 _____ A
_____ B
_____ C
(Title)_____ C

Bridge _____ A
_____ B
_____ C
_____ B

Chorus 2 _____ A
_____ B
_____ C
(Title)_____ C

Verse 3 _____ A
_____ B
_____ C
_____ B

Chorus 3 _____ A
_____ B
_____ C
(Title)_____ C

LYRIC EXAMPLE 9 — Ask a Burning Question

SPECS

Idea: What if God was named "Brent?"

Who's singing: Someone who is posing the question

Reason for the song: The singer is intrigued by the semantic ramifications of the question, and shares his thoughts.

Working title: "Brent is on His Throne"

Song form: Verse/Verse/Bridge/Chorus; Verse/Verse/Chorus/Tag (AABC; AACD)

Rhyme scheme: Verses – ABCB Bridge – ABAA Choruses – AABA Tag – AABA

Title position: The title occupies the 1st and 4th lines of each chorus.

General Word Bank

Name	Real	Trust	Gate
Persona	Bonafide	Plead	Damn
Label	Guarantee	Answer	Willing
Term	Heaven	Mercy	Above
Word	Trinity	Provide	Knows
Called	Angelic	Protect	Created
Pray	Altar	Brent	Given

Word Bank Rhymes

Name: game, shame, fame, flame, tame, same, maim, lame, came, dame, frame

Persona: Kona, Jonah, "kimon-ah," Desdemona, "My Sharona"

Label: cable, table, stable, Betty Grable, fable, gable, (dis)able, Cain and Abel, enable, Mabel, sable, a babe'll

Term: firm, affirm, confirm, berm, squirm, sperm, germ, worm, perm

Word: heard, Kurd, erred, stirred, bird, turd, curd, spurred, third, absurd, inured, deferred, referred, occurred, concurred, chauffeured, conferred, interred

Called: stalled, balled, sprawled, crawled, hauled, mauled, walled, appalled

Pray: bray, day, today, hooray, sway, okay, fray, dismay, way, away, bay, hey, hay, beret, nay, bourré, flambé, oi vey, stay, stray, tray, gray, pay, gay, may, croquet, lamé, say, spray, filet, olé

Real: steal, meal, reel, feel, squeal, peel, peal, appeal, repeal, heel, heal, congeal, deal

Bonafide: codified, Kona tide, boner ride, coincide (loose – bum a ride, coincide, bogus cry, don'cha cry, don'cha hide, so I sighed, sho' 'nuff lie(d), fratricide, homicide, suicide, mortified, horrified, go inside, get inside, go outside, get outside, "apple pied")

Guarantee: free, tea, tee, be, bee, knee, gee, degree, decree, fee, hee-hee, key, me, pee, see, spree, whee, ye, flee, flea, plea, O.D., M.D., OCD, yippee, V.I.P., DDT

Heaven: seven, eleven

Trinity: affinity, magnanimity, divinity, infinity, salinity

Angelic: psychedelic, relic, Tom Selleck (loose – Celtic)

Altar: falter, halter, exalter, exalt 'er, Gibraltar, defaulter, pole vaulter, salt 'er

Trust: bust, cussed, dust, just, lust, fussed, bussed, must, rust, nonplussed (loose – us)

Plead: read, feed, bead, weed, heed, impede, steed, freed, peed, concede, bleed, creed, deed, indeed, precede, proceed, lead, need, weed, speed

Answer: dancer, prancer, cancer, advancer, enhancer (loose stresswise: freelancer)

Mercy: Circe, Percy (loose – Hershey)

Provide: confide, tide, (be)lied, sighed, side, ride, snide, hide, pride, wide, collide, abide, cried, tried, pried, died, complied, denied, fried

Protect: sect, erect, (dis)infect, decked, flecked, (hen)pecked, (in) direct, project, elect, effect, affect, detect, collect, (dis)connect, reject, expect, inspect, select, interject, resurrect, subject, respect, recollect, defect, necked (loose – wreck, check, neck, exec, spec, heck...)

Brent: bent, hell-bent, sent, lent, dent, rent, meant, cent, went, vent, spent, assent, ascent, dissent, descent, event, extent, ferment, repent, relent, prevent, percent, intent, lament, content, (mis)represent, indent, torment, cement, augment, present, consent

Gate: bait, wait, date, late, hate, berate, elate, ate, spate, trait, pate, crate, freight, rate, fate, berate

Damn: cram, dram, gram, ham, jam, Sam, Uncle Sam, Pam, "sha-zam," clam, am, gam, lam, scram, yam, exam, goddamn, Grand Am, Madame, slam, tram, "BLAM," scam, wham, bam (thank you) ma'am, sham, lamb, ram

Willing: billing, shilling, killing, grilling, filling, tilling, drilling, milling, fulfilling

Above: love, glove, of, shove, hereof, thereof, dove

Knows: goes, shows, foes, John Does, hellos, flows, glows, slows, rows, rose, snows, woes, froze, toes, doze, arose, suppose, close, Van Goghs

Created: baited, waited, dated, hated, berated, elated, crated, rated, fated, berated, sated, gold-plated, equated, (in)stated, understated, deflated, inflated (loose – paraded, serenaded, raided, faded, (up)braided)

Given: striven, David Niven, livin', driven

Title Rhymes for "Throne"

Shown, thrown, (be)moan, bone, cone, condone, crone, flown, hone, Saint Joan, phone, stone, zone, sewn, sown, loan, alone, clone, filet mignon, cologne, own, drone, tone, atone, blown, grown, groan, (un)known, disown

EXAMPLE 9

"Brent is on His Throne"

Verse 1   *Kings and queens have given names,*
Like Zoey, Chad or Percy
So why not the guy who created us all
With whom we plead for mercy?

Verse 2   *Jesus doesn't really count*
He's just number two in the Trinity
There's Father, Son and Holy Ghost
Let's focus on Daddy Divinity

Bridge   *What if God was named Brent?*
Oh my Brent, that's awesome
Though it sounds a little bent
I'd love to "let go and let Brent"

Chorus 1   *Brent is on His throne*
He watches o'er His own
A mighty fortress is our Brent
Brent is on His throne

Verse 3   *We hear some talk of "Yahweh"*
But that's a sacred label
So feared that it can't be spoken aloud
Not a handle, like Cain or Abel

Verse 4   *Now, "Brent" we can relate to*
Ev'ry time we're in a jam
When we get sad or broke or sick,
That guy will give a damn

Chorus 2   *Brent is on His throne*
We'll never be alone
Because we must, in Brent we trust
Brent is on His Throne

Tag   *When you're scared of the unknown*
When hopes and dreams have flown
Remember who looks out for you
Brent is on His throne

In these lyrics my thematic line became a statement, even though the song idea is a question. Your own thematic line in Puzzle #9 might well be something that ends with a question mark. A tag is always an option with any song. I've included them in #9 and #11; they can be any rhyme scheme you want – if possible, I encourage you to conclude with the title.

LYRIC PUZZLE 9   Ask a Burning Question

Idea: _____

Who's singing: _____

Reason for the song: _____

Working title: _____

Song form: Verse/Verse/Bridge/Chorus; Verse/Verse/Chorus/Tag (AABC; AACD)
Rhyme scheme: Verses – ABCB   Bridge – ABAA   Choruses – AABA   Tag – AABA
Title position: The title occupies the 1st and 4th lines of each chorus.

1. Create a General Word Bank.

2. Create a list of Word Bank Rhymes.

3. Create a list of Title Rhymes for _____.

"Working Title"

Verse 1 _____ A
        _____ B
        _____ C
        _____ B

Verse 2 _____ A
        _____ B
        _____ C
        _____ B

Bridge _____ A
        _____ B
        _____ A
        _____ A

Chorus 1 (Title)_____ A
        _____ A
        _____ B
        (Title)_____ A

Verse 3 _____ A
        _____ B
        _____ C
        _____ B

Verse 4 _____ A
        _____ B
        _____ C
        _____ B

Chorus 2 (Title)_____ A
        _____ A
        _____ B
        (Title)_____ A

Tag _____ A
        _____ A
        _____ B
        (Title)_____ A

LYRIC EXAMPLE 10 Give Advice

Idea: Don't give advice (that's my advice).*

Who's singing: Someone who seems to have learned this the hard way

Reason for the song: The singer implores others to learn from his/her experience.

Working title: "Never, Ever Give Advice"

Song form: Verse/Verse/Chorus; Verse/Verse/Chorus; Bridge/Chorus (AAB; AAB; CB)

Rhyme scheme: Verses – ABCB   Choruses – ABCC   Bridge – ABCB

Title position: The title concludes each chorus.

General Word Bank

Ask	Opine	Aware	Say
Opinion	Offend	Life	Hurt
Truth	Aback	Confidante	Reform
Sincere	Intention	Tell	Change
Counsel	Best	Confide	Heart
Friend	Pal	Reveal	Clarity
Viewpoint	Knows	News	True

Word Bank Rhymes

Ask: task, bask, cask, mask, flask

Opinion: dominion, minion, pinion (loose – Abyssinian, Sardinian, obsidian)

Truth: uncouth, booth, sooth, forsooth, tooth, vermouth, sleuth, Ruth, youth

Sincere: here, beer, seer, tear, veer, we're, leer, peer, rear, queer, near, clear, chandelier, chanticleer, steer, career, endear, dear, fear, drear', tier, pier

Counsel: council, an ounce'll

Friend: offend, send, append, lend, tend, mend, apprehend, comprehend, bend, extend

Viewpoint: new point, true point, boo-hoo-point

Opine: wine, combine, dine, fine, Auld Lang Syne, sign, (mis)align, nine

---

*Inspired by this quote from Oscar Wilde: *"It is always a silly thing to give advice, but to give good advice is absolutely fatal."*

Offend: apprehend, mend, send, lend, tend, bend, extend, comprehend, append, ascend, descend, blend, penned, pretend

Aback: crack, shack, tack, clickety-clack, slack, pack, rack, flak, attack, hack, jack

Intention: invention, absention, declension, tension, mention, detention, intervention, convention, suspension, condescension, pretension, pension, ascension

Best: pest, rest, nest, zest, west, behest, fest, guest, jest, blessed, confessed, crest

Pal: gal, locale, corral, bacchanal, Al, morale, femme fatale, musicale

Knows: goes, shows, foes, John Does, hellos, flows, expose, glows, slows, snows, froze, doze, disclose, beaux, faux, bows, rows, rose, nose, hose, close, Van Goghs

Aware: dare, fair, share, au pair, declare, (for)swear, stare, glare, rare, lair, spare, prayer, wear, where, there, hair, tear, square, flare, flair, stair

Life: wife, strife, knife, rife, fife, Barney Fife

Confidante: au courant, font, croissant, savant, en passant, want (loose – gaunt, haunt, flaunt, aunt, taunt, contretemps)

Tell: shell, hell, sell, bell, mademoiselle, Estelle, rebel, repel, compel, gazelle, (be)fell, gel, quell, smell, spell, well, yell, dispel, hotel, motel, noel, Muscatel, swell

Confide: tide, (be)lied, sighed, side, ride, snide, hide, pride, wide, collide, abide, cried, tried, pried, died, complied, provide, denied, fried

Reveal: seal, kneel, squeal, feel, meal, peel, peal, deal, heal, congeal, steal, weal, zeal

News: who's/whose, cruise, snooze, sues, moos, ooze, lose, pews, Jews, peruse, excuse, eschews, blues, dues, views, zoos, (mis)use, cues

Say: bray, day, today, hooray, sway, okay, fray, dismay, way, away, bay, hay, beret, nay, bourre, flambé, oi vey, stay, stray, tray, pray, gray, fiancée, pay, gay, may

Hurt: shirt, flirt, curt, blurt, quirt, subvert, avert, dirt, alert, pert, squirt, inert, overt, covert

Reform: dorm, storm, norm, swarm

Change: mange, grange, range, strange, arrange

Heart: start, cart, mart, tart, a la carte, part, dell Sartre, art, dart, fart, depart, apart, (out)smart

Clarity: rarity, disparity, parity, hilarity, polarity, popularity, solidarity, singularity, similarity, vulgarity, familiarity, peculiarity (loose – parody, merrily, warily, scarily)

True: blue, boo-hoo, new, anew, coo, coup, do, doo-doo, who, zoo, moo, screw, to, too, drew, Jew, blew, crew, pooh-pooh, sue (loose – crude, conclude, rude, nude…)

Title Rhymes for "Advice"

Twice, price, nice, spice, thrice, suffice, lice, dice, mice, rice, precise, device, slice, ice, splice, entice, Heidi Fleiss, concise, Anne Rice, vise, vice (in a pinch – "paradise," even though the accent is wrong and it truly doesn't rhyme. Note to self: don't use it. "Pair of dice" is good…)

EXAMPLE 10

"Never, Ever Give Advice"

Verse 1
Don't tell your wife she looks fat in those jeans
Resist that intervention
Suggesting a muu-muu with vertical stripes
Will only result in tension

Verse 2
So what if Grandpa has bad breath
And everybody knows it?
Offer mints at every turn
But don't you dare disclose it

Chorus 1
No one wants to hear the truth
Keep them in the dark
Better to be nice
Never, ever give advice

Verse 3
When Emily asks your viewpoint
On her prissy fiancée
Say she's picked a winner
Even though you're sure he's gay

Verse 4
When Joe takes up the violin
In search of a career
Dab a happy hanky to your eye
And try to look sincere

Chorus 2
No one wants to hear the truth
Keep it to yourself
It isn't worth the price
Never, ever give advice

Bridge
Be careful with your counsel
Forget that you know best
Lest you send your loved ones into
Cardiac arrest

Chorus 3
No one wants to hear the truth
Reveal it at your peril
Let me be precise
Never, ever give advice

In these lyrics I like starting each chorus with "No one wants to hear the truth," though you might suspect we have two thematic lines. Well, we do indeed...however, **"Never, ever give advice" stands out as the title because it's rhymed, and it concludes each chorus.** You can have more than one thematic, recurring lyrical element as long as it doesn't confuse the point of the song.

LYRIC PUZZLE 10 Give Advice

SPECS

Idea: _____

Who's singing: _____

Reason for the song: _____

Working title: _____

Song form: Verse/Verse/Chorus; Verse/Verse/Chorus; Bridge/Chorus (AAB; AAB; CB)
Rhyme scheme: Verses – ABCB   Choruses – ABCC   Bridge – ABCB
Title position: The title concludes each chorus.

1. Create a General Word Bank.

2. Create a list of Word Bank Rhymes.

3. Create a list of Title Rhymes for _____.

"Working Title"

Verse 1 _____ A
       _____ B
       _____ C
       _____ B

Verse 2 _____ A
       _____ B
       _____ C
       _____ B

Chorus 1 _____ A
        _____ B
        _____ C
        (Title)_____ C

Verse 3 _____ A
       _____ B
       _____ C
       _____ B

Verse 4 _____ A
       _____ B
       _____ C
       _____ B

Chorus 2 _____ A
        _____ B
        _____ C
        (Title)_____ C

Bridge _____ A
      _____ B
      _____ C
      _____ B

Chorus 3 _____ A
        _____ B
        _____ C
        (Title)_____ C

LYRIC EXAMPLE ![11] Tell a Funny Story in the Third Person

SPECS

Idea: A woman has a ridiculously rough day.

Who's singing: Someone who heard about it from someone else who heard about it…

Reason for the song: We hope that somebody who hears this story might realize that their own day isn't going all that badly.

Working title: "She Got Up on the Wrong Side of the Bed"

Song form: Verse/Verse/Chorus; Verse/Verse/Chorus; Bridge/Chorus/Tag (AAB; AAB; CBD)

Rhyme scheme: Verses – ABCB Choruses – ABCB Bridge – ABCB Tag – ABCB

Title position: The title concludes the choruses and the tag.

General Word Bank

(What I've done here is imagine ordinary things, with possible "difficulty words" thrown in…because this is the tale of someone's day. I'll use these words to make up an obstacle-ridden story.)

Woke up	Bank	No!	Fire
Toast	Store	Street	Pain
Cereal	Cop	Crazy	Die
Juice	(Un)lucky	Driver	Tragic
Tribune	Lunch	Shout	Ending
Disaster	Fight	Car	
Trouble	Neighbor	Trip	
Bad	Cleaners	Wild	
Situation	Volunteer	Party	
Gym	Job	Dinner	

Word Bank Rhymes

Woke up: cup, sup, pup, schtup, "ten-hup," yup (Or, different stress – SOAK up, BROKE up, STOKE up, COKE up, TOKE up – i.e., rhyme both sounds.)

Toast: roast, boast, host, coast, ghost, post, almost (Toaster: roaster, coaster, poster)

Cereal: ethereal, funereal, imperial

Juice: noose, caboose, loose, chartreuse, moose, goose, sluice, Bruce, Zeus

Tribune: boon, raccoon, moon, June, spittoon, rune, tune, cartoon, dune, soon, prune, buffoon, strewn, hewn, maroon, spoon (loose – wound, marooned, whom, boom, doom)

Disaster: faster, caster, vaster, plaster, Missus Astor, master, pastor, passed'er, last 'er

Trouble: bubble, rubble, double, stubble

Bad: mad, sad, "rad," pad, tad, Brad, lad, cad, dad, had, ad, add, glad, egad, grad

Situation: consternation, aberration, nation, altercation, vacation, elation, invitation, jubilation, equation, libation, station, trepidation, liberation, sensation, abdication

Gym: him, limb, prim, dim, whim, rim, brim, trim, hymn

Bank: dank, crank, flank, wank, skank, blank, plank, swank, yank, thank, drank, sank, rank, tank, stank, point-blank, franc

Store: bore, core, door, for, four, gore, whore, more, galore, soar, tore, wore, ignore, what-for, Christian Dior, pour, pore, outdoor, corps, floor, adore, your, furthermore, swore, foreswore, oar, score, deplore, before, roar, boar, snore

Cop: bop, cop, shop, drop, pop, swap, top, hop, hip hop, plop, crop, mop, prop

(Un)lucky: ducky, plucky, "Bucky," Kentucky, sucky, yucky, mucky

Lunch: bunch, crunch, punch, hunch, munch, scrunch, brunch

Fight: bite, kite, tight, might, sight, plight, quite, sprite, delight, white, night, fright

Neighbor: saber, (be)labor (loose – favor, savor, paver, behavior, waver, waiver)

Cleaners: wieners, misdemeanors, trampoliners, sweet sixteeners, submariners

Volunteer: beer, cheer, dear, hear, jeer, fear, gear, chandelier, queer, sheer, tear, rear

Job: bob, squab, fob, gob, blob, "no prob'," cob, mob, lob, knob, sob, rob, throb

No!: Joe, blow, hoe, ho', show, know, go, woe, pro, status quo, low, glow, to and fro, crow, snow, John/Jane Doe, chateau, chapeau, tableau, beau, so, sow, slow

Street: beat, compete, delete, neat, sweet, complete, feat, feet, seat, DEET, meat, treat, elite, concrete, bleat, heat, sheet, peat, discreet, repeat, suite, eat, deceit, tweet-tweet

Crazy: hazy, lazy, daisy

Driver: diver, jiver, conniver, fiver, survivor, reviver (loose – buyer, hire, tire, flyer...)

Shout: clout, tout, about, route, spout, doubt, out, bout, draught, sprout, stout, pout, lout

Car: bar, star, tar, far, afar, bizarre, bazaar, armoire, disbar, spar, scar, film noir, jar, ajar

Trip: lip, Crip, drip, strip, pip, dip, snip, hip, rip, zip, whip, tip, quip, flip

Wild: child, riled, piled, smiled, filed, mild, styled, beguiled, tiled

Party: smarty, hearty, Havarti, ex parte, commedia del arte, arty (loose – tardy)

Dinner: spinner, grinner, inner, sinner, winner, beginner, skinner

Fire: buyer, ire, hire, fire, choir, liar, lyre, wire, pyre, friar, dire, squire, prior

Pain: rain, bane, gain, strain, main, inane, insane, crane, Dane, reign, lane, obtain, explain, attain, arcane, urbane, brain, Cain, vane, wane, plane, stain, abstain

Die: buy, try, oh my, Dubai, sigh, why, pie, die, hi, high, sky, tie, untie, fry, pry, nigh

Tragic: magic, hemorrhagic

Ending: pending, bending, sending, tending, offending, ascending, attending, befriending, pretending, comprehending

Title Rhymes for "Bed"

Said, unsaid, dead, bred, bread, wed, led, lead, head, thread, tread, ahead, go ahead, stead, instead, shred, sled, zed, red, sped, spread, ill-bred, misread, read, behead, Fred, Grateful Dead, fed, underfed, pre-med, overhead, corn-fed, crossbred, well-read, misled, bled, Club Med

"She Got Up on the Wrong Side of the Bed"

EXAMPLE 11

Verse 1
There was trouble over at Wal-Mart
When she tried to buy a toaster
The cashier swore he recognized her
From a "wanted" poster

Verse 2
Security was summoned
And the awful thing about it
Was her crazy mom who happened in
And didn't help them doubt it

Chorus 1
She shouldn't have bitten her mother
She should have kept her head
But she got up
On the wrong side of the bed

Verse 3
Later she called nine-one-one
On behalf of her upstairs neighbor
Who was big with child and needed a friend
To share the ordeal of labor

Verse 4
She ended up in traction
On a steady morphine drip
The ambulance ran into a bus
On this particular trip

Chorus 2
She shouldn't have ridden along
She should have sent flowers instead
But she got up
On the wrong side of the bed

Bridge
No one came to the hospital
No one eased her woe
She'd left her I.D. at Wal-Mart
They admitted her as Jane Doe

Chorus 3
She shouldn't have left her house that day
At five they pronounced her dead
She just got up
On the wrong side of the bed

Tag
So much business left undone
And tender words unsaid
She never wed, for she got up
On the wrong side of the bed

LYRIC PUZZLE 11 — Tell a Funny Story in the Third Person

SPECS

Idea: _____

Who's singing: _____

Reason for the song: _____

Working title: _____

Song form: Verse/Verse/Chorus; Verse/Verse/Chorus; Bridge/Chorus/Tag (AAB; AAB; CBD)

Rhyme scheme: Verses – ABCB   Choruses – ABCB   Bridge – ABCB   Tag – ABCB

Title position: The title concludes the choruses and the tag.

1. Create a General Word Bank.

2. Create a list of Word Bank Rhymes.

3. Create a list of Title Rhymes for _____.

"Working Title"

Verse 1 _____ A
_____ B
_____ C
_____ B

Verse 2 _____ A
_____ B
_____ C
_____ B

Chorus 1 _____ A
_____ B
_____ C
(Title)_____ B

Verse 3 _____ A
_____ B
_____ C
_____ B

Verse 4 _____ A
_____ B
_____ C
_____ B

Chorus 2 _____ A
_____ B
_____ C
(Title)_____ B

Bridge _____ A
_____ B
_____ C
_____ B

Chorus 3 _____ A
_____ B
_____ C
(Title)_____ B

Tag _____ A
_____ B
_____ C
(Title)_____ B

LYRIC EXAMPLE **12** Give Advice to a Child

SPECS

Idea: Always remember to brush.

Who's singing: A friend or family member of the child

Reason for the song: We encourage a good habit by way of a cute song.

Working title: "Ya Gotta Brush, Brush, Brush Your Teeth"

Song form: Verse/Verse/Chorus; Verse/Verse/Chorus (AAB; AAB)

Rhyme scheme: Verses – AABB Choruses – ABBA

Title position: The title occupies the 1st and 4th line of each chorus.

General Word Bank

(These words are very simple and straightforward. This is not a satire of a children's song – if it were, we would be more sophisticated about it.)

Clean	Sleepy	Sink
Shiny	Day	Scrub
Bright	Eat	Bed
Great	Cavity	Silly
"Toofies"	Good	Smile
Morning	Mom	Choppers
Noon	Grin	Chew

Word Bank Rhymes

Clean: bean, keen, teen, between, seen

Shiny: tiny, sunshiny, whiny

Bright: night, light, might, delight, right, all right, sight, bite

Great: mate, gate, late, state, first-rate, plate, straight

"Toofies:" goofies

Morning: No rhymes here. "Warning" and "mourning" don't interest us for these lyrics.

Noon: soon, moon, loon, raccoon, balloon, tune, June

Sleepy: sheep-y, weepy, teepee

Day: stay, hey, decay, come what may, hay, Okay, A-Okay

Eat: can't be beat, tweet-tweet, neat, sweet, treat

Cavity: gravity, Macavity

Good: should, could, would, understood

Mom: prom, pom-pom

Grin: been, in, pin, spin, Rin-tin-tin, win

Sink: drink, rinky-tink, blink, pink, shrink, plink, wink, think

Scrub: tub, bub, rub-dub-a-dub

Bed: head, sleepy head, said, instead, read, bread

Silly: willy-nilly, Billy, lily

Smile: mile, awhile, style

Choppers: shoppers, hip hoppers, eye poppers, showstoppers, grasshoppers, toppers

Chew: (brand) new, blue, who, few, do, too, grew

(We don't need title rhymes because we're not going to rhyme the title in the choruses.)

EXAMPLE 12

"Ya Gotta Brush, Brush, Brush Your Teeth"

Verse 1   *You've got a beautiful grin*
The best that's ever been
Your super duper choppers
Are definitely showstoppers!

Verse 2   *So every time you eat*
Or have a sugary treat
(Child's name), what do you think?
Time to head for the bathroom sink!

Chorus 1   *Ya gotta brush, brush, brush your teeth*
Startin' when you're tiny
So they'll always be sunshiny
Ya gotta brush, brush, brush your teeth

Verse 3   *Unless you've got the goofies*
You'll rub-dub-a-dub those "toofies"
You'll have a happy mom
And your picture on smile-dot-com!

Verse 4   *No matter what you chew*
Your teeth can look like new
Don't be "hesitate-y"
Just grab your toothbrush, matey!

Chorus 2   *Ya gotta brush, brush, brush your teeth*
At least three times a day
So they'll be A-okay
Ya gotta brush, brush, brush your teeth

LYRIC PUZZLE **12** Give Advice to a Child

SPECS

Idea: _____

Who's singing: _____

Reason for the song: _____

Working title: _____

Song form: Verse/Verse/Chorus; Verse/Verse/Chorus (AAB; AAB)

Rhyme scheme: Verses – AABB   Choruses – ABBA

Title position: The title occupies the 1st and 4th lines of each chorus.

1. Create a General Word Bank.

2. Create a list of Word Bank Rhymes.

"Working Title"

Verse 1   _____   A
          _____   A
          _____   B
          _____   B

Verse 2   _____   A
          _____   A
          _____   B
          _____   B

Chorus 1   (Title)_____   A
          _____   B
          _____   B
          (Title)_____   A

Verse 3   _____   A
          _____   A
          _____   B
          _____   B

Verse 4   _____   A
          _____   A
          _____   B
          _____   B

Chorus 2   (Title)_____   A
          _____   B
          _____   B
          (Title)_____   A

Congratulations in advance! When you've finished doing each of the preceding assignments, you will definitely know your way around writing funny lyrics. In the next chapter we'll talk about acquiring expertise with other kinds of song forms and rhyme schemes, and of course, creating your own.

7

Write Like the Wind

Expert Departure from the Basics

Said basics:

a. Common rhyme schemes
b. Traditional organization and treatment of verses, choruses, bridges and tags
c. Song-title repetition in proven, winning positions

Can you depart from these basics and still proceed successfully? Of course you can, but do me a favor and start by retaining a disciplined approach, as follows:

Look at any song as a possible model for what you might write (and make funny!). Notice where rhymes occur or don't, where the title is positioned and what the overall song form seems to be.

Here are some lyrics to which I referred in Chapter 1, under "songs that entertain children." This song doesn't conform to the rhyme patterns we've worked with, but you certainly won't find it weird. Let's look at it and see what's there.

"That's How Long I'll Love You"

I'll love you 'til the lolli-pops	A
The honey combs and the flower shops	A
'Til mattress springs and napkin rings	B *(includes internal rhyme)*
That's how long I'll love you	C *(thematic tag line)*
I'll love you 'til the candle sticks	A
The buffalo hide and the pancake mix	A
'Til kettle drums and cookie crumbs	B *(includes internal rhyme)*
That's how long I'll love you	C *(thematic tag line)*
'Til coconut flakes and thick milk shakes	A *(includes internal rhyme)*
'Til Tootsie Rolls and ice cream bowls	B *(includes internal rhyme)*
'Til twisty-ties and butter flies	C *(includes internal rhyme)*
How long do you think I'll love you?	D *(variation of thematic tag line)*
I'll love you 'til Niag'ra Falls	A
'Til micro-waves and wild duck calls	A
'Til sausage links and the kitchen sinks	B *(includes internal rhyme)*
That's how long I'll love you	C *(thematic tag line)*

The song form above is Verse/Verse/Bridge/Verse…the title is used thematically but is never set up to rhyme; it just stabilizes the song…notice that the patterns in the verses are consistent, and the bridge presents a contrast by varying the rhyme scheme and the thematic line.

More thematicism is created by the repetition of "I'll love you" and "'til," again and again. And of course the overall theme is that I've implied a collection of crazy "verbs" that aren't really verbs. It's a nonsense song, but its construction is far from nonsensical.

At this point you have quite sufficient know-how to examine any song you want and determine its lyrical roadmap. If you like it, grab it! But remember this:

> If you need to create material that's expected to be original, any emulation might be obvious if your model song is too overly-well-known for its clever rhyme layout. Case in point:

> "Let's Call the Whole Thing Off" by Cole Porter
> (*"You say potato, and I say po-tah-to…"*)

> If you were to duplicate this song's form and rhyme patterns, it would sound too much like the original for comfort. If you're out to do a parody, then no problem…

Parodies

We touched upon these in Chapter 2, when we revisited "Mary Had a Little Lamb." Once again, a parody is an imitation of an existing, well known work – usually for the purpose of spoofing or satirizing it. It could also be just for the hell of it.

A parody equals alteration of a major element of the original (famous) thing, while something else is left intact. For example, one might:

a. Change the words to a song, but not the music.

b. Change the music to a song, but not the words.

c. Change most of the words in a poem but make sure that the audience still knows what you're parodying – for example, people love to parody "'Twas the Night Before Christmas."

    d. Add lyrics to famous music where none existed before.*

Parodies do make audiences laugh, and you may well want to write them. Just substitute your crazy lyrics for the originals and keep the well known melody. Search for parodies on the internet and you'll find countless examples.

Be Careful of the Length of a Composition

Beginners often come up with too many lyrics for just one song, and hope to squeeze them all in. Avoid this by working within the song forms we've practiced, or by patterning your construction after other well-written songs of your choice.

A finished song is, of course, its own little show. Milton Berle said, *"An 'act' is a presentation with a beginning, middle and end."* Craft your lyrics to follow exactly the road you want the audience to travel. When a song or a show accomplishes its ultimate magic trick, it leaves the audience satisfied that it was "enough," yet they wish there had been even more. They should enjoy the conclusion, but regret it just a little!

Off the Beaten Path

Actors and writers come to me regularly with ideas for musical material landing outside the parameters I've shown you:

    a. Multiple characters singing opposing views in spurts of various numbers of lines – a shared song that may go so far as to resemble a kind of opera

---

*"Hello Muddah, Hello Faddah" by Allan Sherman, is written to the tune of Ponchielli's "Dance of the Hours." You may have heard this music in Disney's *Fantasia*.

b. "Sung monologues" that may rhyme unpredictably or not at all

c. Pieces involving sung lines or sections, mixed with spoken lines

I love this stuff when it has a great reason to be realized, though it's more complicated to work with than your traditional "song."

If you're inclined to write in these directions, **work above all to conceive your lyrics in a rhythmic way that is clear and pleasing**. That way they will be able to live easily in a musical environment.

You want your words to merge with music, and music must flow or it isn't music. That doesn't mean it can't stop, start, slow down or speed up; however, it must somehow dance in the air – not careen out of control. If what you write fits well into some sort of rhythmic collage, it *can* work musically.

Always look carefully to see if your work can be improved by leaning toward tried-and-true rhyming patterns and sectional organization of songs. For example, if you've got two performers singing a conversation, it might make wonderful sense for them to sing two lines each, back and forth, in a perceivable rhyme scheme. (Or this may not work for the effect you want, but…consider it.)

If you're a composer as well as a lyricist, you can be in charge of the whole outcome and truly write anything you like. This book presumes that you write words but not necessarily music, and has generally sought to prepare you to work with composers – the subject of the next chapter!

8

Do I Hear a Waltz?

How to Work with a Composer

Any composer will be pleased to run into *you*, a lyricist who understands how to write words that can be readily set to music. Plus you're about to bring some laughs into the room! The more smoothly your lyrics fit into sections that are typical of songs in general, the easier it will be for someone to create good melodies for them.

What about the fact that your lyrics are funny? Does that impact composition of music? It definitely does.

You want to work with a composer who shares your sense of what's absurd. The musical treatment of your lyrics can have a significant effect upon what you accomplish comedically.

You also want a composer who can write the kind of music you want to hear, whether by musical specialty or just plain versatility.

Let's say that your song is a satire of an eighties power ballad (i.e., "Total Eclipse of the Heart"); you want the music to sound just like that, so that the exaggerated, ridiculous words live in the proper context. The right composer will also be capable of going further – caricaturing the needed musical style in order to enhance the funny.

On occasion you'll want to go for "musical incongruity" to boost the humor of a song. If the title is "I Lost My Lollipop Last Night," it might be funny for the music to be sultry and stripper-esque, even if the lyrics are childlike. If you have this in mind, the composer should be able to see your point.

It's not necessary to agree on every little thing – just the big stuff. You want to be on the same wavelength. If a composer doesn't think your lyrics are funny and you're certain that they are, you should find someone else to work with.

The specific nature of your collaboration will depend upon the task at hand. Here are some typical situations:

You Have Some Kind of Melody for Your Lyrics

How "done" is the tune of your song? Do you already have a kind of tune in mind, and therefore a style? (The character and feel of even a vague melody will suggest a musical style.) If you do have a tune and can sing it, plan to make a simple recording of this for the composer to use as a reference when you're not around.

Giving your lyrics a melody should be the number one thing to get done in a way you like. Minus any accompaniment, such as guitar or piano, you need a tune that works; one that feels appropriate and is highly singable.

If you have a very well developed idea of a tune for your lyrics, you obviously don't need someone to create a melody from zero;

however, any composer might have thoughts about how to refine or improve upon what you've got. The less you know about music, the more open-minded you should be about this. You may get some very welcome assistance.

After melody comes harmony, meaning "chords." When chords are selected to accompany a melody, we say that it is "harmonized." Any tune can be potentially supported by some wide variety of chords. Which chords end up being chosen will determine a great deal about how a song comes across when it's heard.

What if you don't know a thing about chords? Don't worry. That's why you're paying a musician *an unfathomable sum* to help out (contact me anytime).

Capable guitarists or piano players will be able to concoct logical chords for a song rather immediately if the melody makes sense. This is not genius, though it may look like that to you. Good melodies have much in common with each other, and musicians become accustomed to which chord progressions will work in a flash. Even so, don't hesitate to point out the brilliance of your composer every few minutes.

Meanwhile, there is a good chance that the first go-round will not succeed in producing chords that you consider perfect. Experiment – go shopping.

"That's not quite what I had in mind – can you show me something *jazzier, warmer, darker, happier?* (Avoid use of the word "better" as an adjective here.) Your musical vocabulary may not be vast, but all artists respond to imagery and sensuality, so talk away...

When harmonizing a tune, there is always some picking and choosing involved. You'll like "this chord but not that one." This is par for the course, so don't feel badly about shooting for what you truly like. There will be an eventual, mutual agreement between you and a composer about what works well, unless you are a nut case or possess a complete absence of musical taste. (A reverse situation is also possible. When you meet with a composer, be sure to retain an initial awareness of exit routes.)

You Have No Melody for Your Lyrics

Are you hearing your lyrics in rhythm, with some sort of speed or musical feel built in, but no melody at all? That's perfectly fine and not uncommon – in this case you're a wordsmith in need of a composer to help create a melody where none yet exists.

When your concept of the song at hand is solely rhythmic, a composer needs to understand exactly how you're hearing the lyrics move through time. You should do one of the following, or both:

1. Make a recording of yourself reciting the lyrics in rhythm. I suggest snapping your fingers or clapping lightly throughout this presentation. When I work with lyricists as a composer, I often encounter a tendency for them to rush through the spaces between words or phrases here and there, basically "skipping beats."

The usual reason for this is that they're hurrying things along as a kind of time saver. It's actually the opposite of a time saver, because it requires extra effort and discussion for me to figure out how they really want the song to go.

When you make a recording to demonstrate how your song lives in time, be as "musical" as you personally can. It's okay if you're not flawless, just avoid hurrying and communicate what's in your head.

2. Make a copy of your lyrics for the composer to keep. I want you to do this in a specific way, because the **flow of words** you intend is not always clear to another person from reading lyrics on a page. This rhythmic flow may even seem clear to someone else, yet it's not what you meant. Here's how to fix that – put syllables or words in CAPS that you want stressed. Compare the examples below:

   a. *There was this brilliant lyricist*
      Who couldn't pay the rent
      Her words were swell but it was hell
      To tell how the damn things went

   b. *There WAS this brilliant LYricist*
      Who COULDn't pay the RENT
      Her WORDS were SWELL but IT was HELL
      To TELL how the damn things WENT

The first version above with no caps seems pretty clear, but the caps make the major beats absolutely unmistakable. (You could instead mark your lyrics with a highlighter.) It will often be impossible to show all the lyrical rhythms you want with only the written word; nevertheless, this kind of document will help show a composer how your lyrics are intended to flow.

If anything still seems problematic, the composer will point it out and suggest a solution. Possible situations: too many syllables in a line of lyrics...odd use of a word with regard to the way it's pronounced (spoken, sung!).

But let's say that your lyrics are fine; eminently eligible for marriage to a melody. Now is the time to tell a composer the musical style you want, or confer and agree upon one that makes sense for the song.

A great way for you to contribute your views to this process is to offer examples of well known songs that demonstrate the style you have in mind. *"I was thinking along the lines of 'Hit Me with Your Best Shot.'"* You may want to bring a recording. It's very easy for someone who writes music to compose original material that is "similar to XYZ but not XYZ."

Now you're on the road to having the right melody for your words. This becomes a homework assignment for your composer – don't ask for it to happen right on the spot, except in a form of a general facsimile.

When the time comes for you to hear a "draft" of the finished song, the composer will have combined melody and chords in order to play it for you, recorded or live. Every aspect of this product is now discussable and malleable. Point out what you like or don't, and present reasons for your opinions as best you can. No one can work with criticism that consists only of "it just doesn't sit right." As I mentioned previously, don't worry about speaking in musical terms – express yourself freely and communication is likely to be successful.

You Play Guitar or Keyboard and Have Created a Melody and Accompaniment for Your Song

Why would you need a composer's help? The following reasons could exist:

1. You don't know how to turn the song into sheet music, and would like someone to write it down. You need one of the following:

    a. A lead sheet (lyrics, melody and chord symbols)

    b. A piano arrangement

    c. An instrumental arrangement for some combination of musicians

    d. A vocal arrangement involving more than one singer

If you additionally want any of the above to be performed and recorded, and don't know how to proceed, a composer will be able to help you with that, too.

2. You think that the music for your song needs improvement, and are seeking help. Be especially careful if you're paying money. Only work with a composer that you're sure is good at the kind of material you're doing. Get trusted referrals, ask for demos to listen to – search the internet. Talk on the phone to prospective partners and go with someone you like personally. You want to have fun working together.

In Conclusion

I invite you to wind down now, right along with me. This is the end of my
third book in a series, each of them related to music and comedy. Does
the world need more funny stuff? Always. People thirst for humor…it's
the saving grace of many a day. Laughter even has an afterglow: *"Wow, I
haven't laughed like that in a long time."* I think it's a great thing to work
diligently toward the creation of that experience.

I'm privileged to be friends with legendary composer and lyricist, Richard
M. Sherman, who wrote: *"In every job that must be done there is an element of fun; you find the fun, and snap! The job's a game!"* The contents
of this book represent a game – a way to play at making up funny lyrics.
For me this makes the task enjoyable to do over and over again.

It's quite possible to write comic lyrics from start to finish by chewing on the
end of a pencil, staring into space and seeing what comes to you. When
that's productive, I'm all for it. Meanwhile, I'm hoping that my little strate-
gies, lists and procedures will prove handy for you as creative stimuli.

Live comedy shows often feature songs that satirize the topical: items in
the news, today's politicians and celebrities, any current event. That kind
of material is by nature short-lived because what's current keeps changing.
The techniques I've shared with you will work just fine for that sort of subject matter; however, throughout this book I've intentionally applied song
ideas that won't become dated anytime soon.

Good luck and happy, hilarious writing.

INDEX